Infant Baptism

A Parish Celebration

Font and Table Series

The *Font and Table Series* offers pastoral perspectives on Christian baptism, confirmation and eucharist.

OTHER TITLES IN THE SERIES ARE:

A Catechumenate Needs Everybody: Study Guide for Parish Ministers

At That Time: Cycles and Seasons in the Life of a Christian

Baptism Is a Beginning

The Catechumenate and the Law

Celebrating the Rites of Adult Initiation: Pastoral Reflections

The Church Speaks about Sacraments with Children:
Baptism, Confirmation, Eucharist, Penance

Confirmation: A Parish Celebration

Confirmed as Children, Affirmed as Teens

Finding and Forming Sponsors and Godparents

Guide for Sponsors

How Does a Person Become a Catholic?

How to Form a Catechumenate Team

Issues in the Christian Initiation of Children

One at the Table: The Reception of Baptized Christians

Readings In the Christian Initiation of Children

Welcoming the New Catholic

When Should We Confirm? The Order of Initiation

RELATED AND AVAILABLE THROUGH LITURGY TRAINING PUBLICATIONS:

The Rite of Christian Initiation of Adults (ritual and study editions)

Rito de la Iniciación de Adultos (ritual and study editions)

A Baptism Sourcebook

Catechumenate: A Journal of Christian Initiation

Forum Essays series
  The Role of the Assembly in Christian Initiation
  Eucharist as Sacrament of Initiation
  On the Rite of Election
  Preaching the Rites of Christian Initiation

Infant Baptism

A PARISH CELEBRATION

Timothy Fitzgerald

Liturgy Training Publications

Acknowledgments

All references to the *Rite of Christian Initiation of Adults* are based on the text and paragraph numbers of the 1988 edition: © 1985, International Committee on English in the Liturgy; © 1988, United States Catholic Conference. All rights reserved.

All references to the *Rite of Baptism for Children* are © 1969, International Committee on English in the Liturgy, Inc. All rights reserved.

Copyright © 1994, Archdiocese of Chicago: Liturgy Training Publications, 1800 North Hermitage Avenue, Chicago IL 60622-1101; 1-800-933-1800, FAX 1-800-933-7094. All rights reserved.

Editor: Victoria M. Tufano
Editorial assistance: David Lysik, Jennifer McGeary, Sarah Huck
Design: Kerry Perlmutter
Typesetter: Jim Mellody-Pizzato
Art by Rosie Kelly
Photographs on pages 27, 49, 81 and 93 by Marchita Mauck.
Photographs on pages 15, 41 and 65 by Anne Chadowski.

This book was set in Goudy Old Style.

Printed in the United States of America.

Library of Congress Cataloging-in-Publication Data

Fitzgerald, Timothy, 1950
      Infant baptism: a parish celebration / Timothy
      Fitzgerald.
         110 p. — (Font and table series)
      ISBN 1-56854-008-6 (pbk.)
         1. Infant baptism. 2. Baptism—Catholic Church.
      3. Baptism (Liturgy) 4. Catholic Church—Liturgy.
      I. Title. II. Series.
      BV813.2.58   1994   93-46861
      264'.020812—dc20   CIP

Table of Contents

Introduction

As I write about the liturgical practice of baptizing children, our Midwest region is experiencing the most severe floods in its history. The writing in this summer of 1993 has been framed nearly every day by boiling clouds and heavy rains. In Iowa, where church communities usually ask God for rain in the crucial month of July, the prayers have been for at least one week of dry weather, at least one day of sunshine. People have been driven from their homes, losing everything. Crops have been ruined on hundreds of farms, and the harvest elsewhere this fall will be greatly diminished.

The waters have been relentless and chaotic. We have discovered again that the waters are not easily tamed.

The city of Des Moines and several of its suburbs lost their water system for nearly two weeks when floodwaters topped 25-foot levees and swamped the waterworks. It has been a strange and humbling experience for the 250,000 people affected: lining up for drinking water, collecting rainwater, using the portable toilets, taking dirty children and dirty laundry to the grandparents' home across the state—and all of this during torrential rains.

It's been a little schizophrenic: We are surrounded by water, and at the very same time we are out of water.

The rhythms and patterns of life for all of us have been disrupted. The whole community has been out of sync. We joke about it, we talk about it, we complain about it, we go along with it, we try to make sense out of this chaos. Like Norman Maclean in *A River Runs Through It*, we are haunted by waters in these days.

The waters bring destruction, while our dry faucets remind us of how we depend upon water for health. It is a potent and ambiguous force. It can be both blessing and curse. Under control and in regular amounts, it is life itself for us. Out of control, it ignores us and answers only to God. A simple glass of water has been a precious commodity this summer, a real luxury. But that same water killed and drowned and wreaked havoc.

We toy with the ambiguity of this mighty force when we recount the stories of our family—the great story of life that sprang from the primal waters of chaos; the rescue of our ancestors, saved from certain death only by God leading them safely through the waters; the story of Jesus dunked into the Jordan River and emerging as the Chosen One who was chosen to die. We tell these stories, as count-less generations before us have, to learn again the great lesson of trust: These waters bear life and death both, and only the hand of God rules over them. Only God brings life out of chaos, only God rescues when all else fails, only God brings victory out of apparent defeat. And only by God's mighty hand are all who pass through the waters saved from drowning and raised to life.

Then we reenact this mighty rescue, this cosmic act of creation, by guiding people through the baptizing waters. On behalf of God, we do what God has done for our ances-tors: We draw the person through the dangerous waters and declare that they have new life. Now you are like the Israelites, we proclaim, rescued from certain death and led forth to freedom. Now you are like Christ, chosen for special duty and bound for glory.

You'd think we would know by now what this simple action means. It has been repeated by Christians world-wide for 20 centuries. It is repeated millions of times each year, in rivers and swimming pools, indoors and outside, in miniature bowls and in flowing fonts. It has a thousand variations, enacted by full-body immersion or by dunking or with a dribble on the head. But in fact there are as many meanings to this simple action as there are ways to

perform it. We Catholics thought we had the one defini-
tive meaning of it, but our historical searching and the
reform of our rites have shown us the meaning is as potent
and ambiguous—and as hard to control—as the water
we use.

So we repeat this simple action over and over, not because
we already know what it means. No, we repeat this action
of passage and birth so that we will gradually learn what it
means. We had so tamed the waters that we thought the
action meant only one thing: Before the baptizing there
was only sin, then after the baptizing there was grace. We
convinced ourselves the waters meant this and only this.
But when we started to study our history and redo our ritual, we loosed the waters.

And we have discovered again that the waters are not so
easily tamed. The safe practices and smug answers about
baptism have given way to practices more potent and
ambiguous and to new answers and new questions.

Even the face of the church that baptizes has been affected.
Before, there was only the baptism of infants and the
secret baptism for the occasional adult. Now, insulated
parishes are becoming evangelizing parishes; there is the
public invitation and initiation of thousands of adults,
and the presence in our midst once again of catechumens.
And only in that greater context of adult faith is there
initiation of children, only one part of which is baptism.

What do these waters mean? What does this simple act of
passage mean? Now we know it means lots of things, and
it reminds us of lots of passages we all have made and
will make. One thing we see and understand better than
before: These waters are always dangerous, to be feared,
almost out of control. We forget that at our own risk.
But something wonderful will happen here, because that
strong and surprising hand of God will transform these
waters and this passage through them into a source of life
for all who gather. And when we witness again the safe

passage, we remember that God can give safe passage even through death itself. So we learn to trust once again: "We do believe."

I will never take the waters for granted again.

Chapter 1

THE BEGETTING COMMUNITY

The act of baptizing is essential to the church's life. Proclaiming the Good News in such a way that people are moved to profess faith and be baptized is a charge given to the Christian community from the Risen Christ himself (Matthew 28:16–20). Following the 1974 Synod of Bishops on evangelization, Paul VI emphatically reiterated this: "Evangelizing all people constitutes the essential mission of the church. Evangelizing is her deepest identity. She exists in order to evangelize" (*On Evangelization in the Modern World*, #14). Regis Duffy captures that same truth in more poetic language, calling the church "the begetting community."[1]

This image of church still catches us off guard. Most of us have been schooled to see "The Church" as an organization for the benefit of its loyal members. So, we assumed, "The Church" exists primarily for our sake, to take care of those who belong.

But the revision of our initiatory practices has brought this "begetting," this evangelizing work, this conceiving of new life in Christ, out into the open. Our understanding of the mission of the church has begun to shift and to expand. This more public experience of initiation reveals again the urgency of the Risen Christ's words: "Go . . . make disciples . . . baptizing them . . . teaching them." (Matthew 28:19–20)

No private matter, the initiation of people stands at the very heart of the community's life and existence. The revised rite of initiation is insistent on this:

> The church believes it is her most basic and necessary duty to inspire all, catechumens, parents of children still to be baptized and godparents, to that true and living faith by which they adhere to Christ and enter into or confirm their commitment to the new covenant. (*General Introduction to Christian Initiation* [GI], #3)

Christian instruction and the preparation for baptism are a vital concern of God's people, the church, which hands on and nourishes the faith it has received from the apostles. Through the ministry of the church, adults are called by the Holy Spirit to the gospel, and infants are baptized and brought up in this faith. (GI, #7)

THE PEOPLE OF GOD, THE CHURCH

In all the documents that refer to initiation, the first minister of baptism to be listed is the church itself: "God's people, the church" (GI, #7); "the people of God, as represented by the local church" (*Rite of Christian Initiation of Adults* [RCIA], #9); "the people of God, that is, the church" (*Rite of Baptism for Children* [RBC], #4).

> The people of God . . . should understand and show by their concern that the initiation of adults is the responsibility of all the baptized. The community must always be fully prepared in the pursuit of its apostolic vocation to give help to those who are searching for Christ. . . . All the followers of Christ have the obligation of spreading the faith according to their abilities. Hence, the entire community must help the candidates and catechumens throughout the process of initiation. (RCIA, #9)

The intention is certainly clear: Initiation is the responsibility of all the baptized. Initiation belongs to the church because it is the church's very reason for being.

"The people of God, as represented by the local church," is right to give careful attention to the celebration of baptism, because the celebration is a self-portrait of the baptized and anointed community. Baptism is the primal rite for the church; it evokes and conveys our self-identity, the "begetting community" busy creating and nurturing new life.

Of course, the church's ministry of initiation with both adults and children encompasses much more than the ritual moment, and it begins long before baptism. "The initiation of catechumens is a gradual process. . . . The rite of initiation is suited to a spiritual journey. . . . An extended period" (RCIA, #4, 5, 75). Even the baptism of children has to be approached as a process of initiation, "allowing sufficient time to prepare the parents and for planning the actual celebration" (RBC, #7.2).

GENERAL DUTIES OF THE INITIATING COMMUNITY

What is the community's ministry? What is this primary minister of baptism responsible for?

The local community is responsible for a general climate of evangelization and outreach. The revised rites of initiation are helping us return evangelization to the heart of our pastoral life. But until and unless a robust and general sense of "evangelical expansion" permeates parish life, the celebration of baptism for children will continue as an isolated, private ritual.

The implicit and explicit invitations the parish offers to people, the outreach it extends to marginal members, the way that couples and families are greeted when they approach the parish about marriage or about baptism—all these affect the "preparation of the children's parents, the celebration of God's word and the profession of baptismal faith." Such evangelization and outreach includes and implies providing legitimate and appropriate preparation for the parents and family of those to be baptized.

The local community is responsible for hospitality. Contrary to popular opinion, the primary responsibility for hospitality does not rest with the presider but with the community, the assembly. The rite of baptism proclaims,

"The Christian community welcomes you with great joy."
But that welcome is meant to unfold long before the ritual
event itself.

The child's "right to the love and help of the community,"
the parents' and families' right to a welcoming visit, to
"pastoral counsel and prayer" press upon the community
as a whole.

Hospitality is a basic component, an essential ingredient,
of a parish. Its importance to the parish's liturgy and life
cannot be overstated. But simple hospitality still receives
far less attention in Catholic parishes than it deserves. St.
Benedict advised his monks that "All guests who present
themselves are to be welcomed as Christ, for he himself
will say, 'I was a stranger and you welcomed me.'" (*Rule of
Benedict*, #53.1) This is sound advice for the parish community as well. How does the parish say "Welcome" to
new families and households? To both familiar faces and
strangers at the door of the church? Who receives the first
request or phone contact about baptism? How is that person at the door or on the phone treated? How is the regis-
tered or unregistered parishioner dealt with when making
even tentative steps toward baptism for the child?

The general spirit and specific practice of hospitality
directly affect the liturgical life of the parish community.
How well the parish celebrates the baptism of its children,
how communal or private the celebration truly is, how
integral initiation is to the building up of the community—
all are influenced by the parish practicing well the art of
gracious receptivity.

**The local community is responsible for "full, conscious,
and active participation" in the celebration of baptism.**
The rite assumes that the celebration of baptism for children is a public, corporate liturgy of and by and for the
church. It assumes that the community is actively engaged
in the celebration, proclaiming its own baptismal faith.
The "begetting community" is formed in faith when it

experiences itself as a source of new life. The sacrament is intended for the community before it is intended for the individual.

That is why the rite presses the issue of the active participation of the community. "The faith in which the children are baptized is not the private possession of the individual family, but it is the common treasure of the whole church of Christ." (RBC, #4) This is best indicated by the full involvement of the parish community.

Many Christian churches would not think of baptizing a child without the congregation gathered; the idea of a "private baptism" seems to them a contradiction in terms. In Catholic circles, by contrast, there remains discomfort or suspicion about the public celebration of baptisms. We are still growing out of a history that reduced baptism to a private and secretive matter.

In part, the community's responsibility is to provide a full, rich and robust celebration of baptism. This is for the sake of the family, to be sure, but more importantly, it is for the church's own sake—to *experience* baptism as richly as possible in order to *understand* baptism as richly as possible. When the church reduces or impoverishes the ritual experience, the church impoverishes itself and its sacramental understanding. We pay a high price whenever we reduce the community's involvement in or experience of itself baptizing children. It may be the result of good intentions or pastoral sensitivity or the wishes of the family that the community seldom or never participates in the baptism of children. But the community's own "begetting" character, its own baptismal faith and its own understanding of initiation remain malnourished when this happens.

The local community is responsible for providing support and resources to parents, family and children during the rest of the process of initiation. The celebration of baptism marks the beginning of an extended initiatory process for children. The rite is blunt about this: Baptism is incomplete in and of itself.

> Through baptism men and women are incorporated into Christ. . . . Signed with the gift of the Spirit in confirmation, Christians more perfectly become the image of their Lord and are filled with the Holy Spirit. . . . Finally they come to the table of the eucharist. . . . Thus the three sacraments of Christian initiation closely combine to bring the faithful to the full stature of Christ and to enable them to carry out the mission of the entire people of God. (GI, #2)

> To fulfill the true meaning of [baptism], children must be later formed in the faith in which they have been baptized. . . . Christian formation, which is their due, seeks to lead them gradually to learn God's plan in Christ, so that they may ultimately accept for themselves the faith in which they have been baptized. (RBC, #3)

"To lead them gradually . . . so they may ultimately accept for themselves" the baptismal faith: Here begins the story of formation in faith, of household and parish community cooperating in this extended task, of relationships and resources and rites supporting and enlightening the children along the pilgrim way.

It is a long-term commitment both parents and community are expected to make by this baptism. The rite wants there to be no mistake about this. The parents are asked, "Do you clearly understand what you are undertaking?" (RBC, #39) If they are not ready for this extended commitment, this is reason for delaying baptism (RBC, #25).

The commitment also binds the community that baptizes. The community assumes responsibility for the network of relationships, mentors and resources "which combine to bring the faithful to the full stature of Christ and to enable them to carry out the mission of the entire people of God." The health of the community's liturgical life, of its service to the poor, of the formation in faith provided for both young and old, and of its efforts to form a community of disciples bear upon the baptizing community's ability to bring the baptized to maturity.

SPECIFIC DUTIES OF THE INITIATING COMMUNITY

In addition to the general duties and dispositions of the community, several specific duties of the local church are spelled out.

1) The church is to see to the preparation of the children's parents, the celebration of God's word and the profession of baptismal faith (GI, #3).

2) Before and after baptism, "the child has a right to the love and help of the community" (RBC, #4). The community helps provide for the later formation in faith for the children, "which is their due" (RBC, #3).

3) Parents are to be provided "with suitable means [of preparation for the rite of baptism], such as books, instructions and catechisms written for families" (RBC, #5.1).

4) The parish priest or others are to visit these parents and families, "preparing them for the coming celebration by pastoral counsel and common prayer" (RBC, #5.1).

5) During the rite, the community "should take an active part" and "exercise its duty when it expresses its assent . . . after the profession of faith by the parents and godparents" (RBC, #4).

PARENTS

The baptism of children is possible because of the faith of the adult community. Children do not profess faith themselves. "They are baptized *in the faith of the church. This faith is proclaimed for them* by their parents and godparents, who represent both the local church and the whole society of saints and believers." (RBC, #2; emphasis added)

The faith of the children is dependent and incomplete, needing time and support to come to maturity. It is a faith, a journey of initiation, especially dependent on the parents' faith and sincerity. The *Rite of Baptism for Children* traces the central role of the parents' ministry (#5):

> **1)** Before the celebration, "it is of great importance" that parents prepare to "take part in the rite with understanding." This preparation is to take place with assistance from the local church, which also has a stake in this celebration of its common faith.

> **2)** "It is very important that the parents should be present" for the baptism. This may seem like a strange directive, but it makes sense as a corrective to the former practice in which godparents stood in for the parents at the baptism; the mother was often not even present. This directive also highlights the rite's insistence that baptism is dependent on the faith of the adult community.

> **3)** During the celebration itself, the parents "have special parts to play." *The Constitution on the Sacred Liturgy*'s mandate for "full, conscious, and active participation" of all the church in liturgy applies to all the ministers of baptism, especially the parents. They are celebrants[2] both as part of the church and in their specific roles in the liturgical event.

4) If one of the parents is not Christian or not in the Catholic communion, he or she is asked at least to give permission for the baptism and "for the child to be instructed in the faith of its baptism" (RBC, #4).

5) After baptism, "it is the responsibility of the parents, in gratitude . . . and fidelity" to form the child in faith, leading the child to confirmation and to eucharist. "In this duty they are again to be helped . . . by suitable means" (RBC, #5).

The rite envisions that the parents will engage in a long-term process of formation, a process affecting them as well as their children. The parents' own faith is the essential element in the baptism of their children. Baptism is no magical moment or instantaneous salvation or polite social gesture. It is the ritual celebration of the faith of the adult believers, "the faith of the church." The faith of the adults is to be "quickened" and affected by this process of baptizing. The rite calls for growth in faith primarily on the part of the adults, especially the parents, and secondarily on the part of the children. The baptism is intended to affect the community baptizing before affecting those to be baptized.

The rite also envisions that the parents are in relationship with a community of believers. This network of relationships assures the parents of the support and help they need before, during and after the baptism. The celebration of baptism is built on the premise that a nurturing community exists, embracing the parents, the family and the one to be baptized.

Different levels of responsibility are reflected in the rite. Baptism and baptismal faith "belong" to the church. That is an important factor in our pastoral approach to baptism and baptismal preparation. But the baptismal faith and life "belong" to the parents as well. The responsibility for baptismal preparation, for "full, conscious and active"

celebration of the liturgy and for conscientious formation in faith for the children rests squarely on the shoulders of those requesting baptism. The parish community and its ministers are not responsible for that parental level of responsibility, nor can they guarantee, force or demand an "appropriate" or "adequate" response to this parental responsibility as a bargaining chip with baptism. This is the parents' responsibility.

The parish community and its ministers are responsible for support, resources, hospitality, preparation, worthy celebration and follow-up. Adequately meeting these responsibilities is all that most parishes can manage. Parishes and ministers sometimes run into problems when they assume the parents' responsibilities, assume enforcement of those responsibilities or assume "sole ownership" of the entire baptismal process. The community and its ministers are responsible for planting seeds and watering; they are not responsible for making the seeds grow and mature. The parents have their own responsibilities, and their freedom and maturity must be respected.

GODPARENTS

The role of godparent is "a very ancient custom of the church" (GI, #8). In adult initiation, the godparent literally and figuratively stands by the one who is baptized. Beginning during the final preparation for baptism, the godparent's ministry takes place especially after baptism. In the period of mystagogia and beyond, the godparent's role is to "help [the neophyte] persevere in the faith and in his/her life as a Christian" (GI, #8).

In adult initiation, the godparent's relationship is with the newly baptized, as a model of faith and source of support. As the sponsor is to the catechumen, so the godparent is to the neophyte, a flesh-and-blood sign of the church standing with the one being initiated.

In the baptism of children, the role is much the same: helping lead the child "to profess the faith and to show this [faith] by living it" (GI, #8). This ministry of support and witness is really the ministry of the entire church, epitomized in this personal representative.

In infant baptism, however, the godparent's relationship is not with the newly baptized child. In fact, the rite of baptism for children lacks any mention of the godparent relating with the child. Instead, the godparent's relationship clearly is to be with the parents, with the adults on whose faith the child's initiation depends. Even the celebration is explicit about this, for it asks the godparents about supporting and witnessing to the parents rather than to the child: "Are you ready to help these parents in their duty as Christian mothers and fathers?" (RBC, #40)

The godparent helps the parents, who lead the child to profess the faith, and the godparent gives living witness to the parents (GI, #8). After all, "the parents have a more important ministry and role in the baptism of infants than the godparents" (RBC, #5). The godparent is expected to be godparent to the family and household, "added spiritually to the immediate family" (GI, #8), rather than only to the individual child.

This provides a wonderful image of the church into which the child is initiated: adults supporting adults in faith, witnessing to and with one another the faith they proclaim, leading their children into this network of relationships by which Christ is revealed and faith is evoked. In this sense, godparents really do represent "the begetting community": "The godparent is present . . . together with the parents, to profess the church's faith, in which the child is being baptized" (GI, #9).

The person who is to be godparent is expected to be sufficiently mature for this role; to be fully initiated by baptism, confirmation and eucharist; and to be a member of the Catholic church, because this is the community of faith the godparent represents (GI, #10). The rites presume that there will be only one godparent. It is not obligatory that there be two godparents, one male and one female. There *must* be one godparent; there *may* be more than one. "Each child *may* have a godfather and a godmother" (RBC, #6; emphasis added). Gender linkage is not compulsory; it is not even mentioned. A baby girl does not require that the godparent be a woman, nor does a baby boy obligate the parents to choose a man as godparent. Maturity in faith is the more important criterion.

Many times, a family has several people in mind to be the godparent and finds it difficult to choose only one. One pastoral approach, a way for several of these people "to be added spiritually to the immediate family," is to have one "formal" godparent, as the rite requires. This person would participate in the baptism as godparent and be recorded in the parish registry. Then the family may choose others as "informal" godparents, other adults who are "ready to help the parents bring up their child" by their support and witness.

In addition to the Catholic godparent, a "baptized and believing Christian" from another church also may be a *godparent* (if from an Orthodox church) or a *Christian witness* (if from the Protestant churches) (GI, #10).

The *Rite of Christian Initiation of Adults* (#11) describes the ministry of the adult neophyte's godparent, but the description also suits the godparent of the child and family: "to show how to practice the gospel in personal and social life, to sustain [them] in moments of hesitancy and anxiety, to bear witness, and to guide [their] progress in the baptismal life." In both cases, this supporting and witnessing ministry provides the ongoing companionship from which faith emerges.

The image of godparent emerging from the revised rites contrasts sharply with a former understanding. In the rite used until 1969, the godparents were more apparent and active than the parents, and quite literally spoke for the infant:

> Then, addressing the candidate for baptism by name, the priest says: "N., do you wish to be baptized?" The sponsors answer: "I do." Then, while either the godfather or godmother, or both, holds the infant, the priest takes baptismal water and pours it three times.

The godparents—always two, always one male and one female—acted as substitute parents in the rite; often the mother was not even present for the baptism. The godparents were understood as quasi-legal guardians, expected to step in if something happened to the parents, committed to completing the education in faith if the parents could not. They were most often relatives or close family friends, "just in case."

In the current *Rite of Baptism for Children*—the first time in the church's history there is a baptismal rite adapted to the situation of children—the godparent is to be fellow believer, chosen for a relationship with the parents, expected to stand by the adults, committed to growth in faith as an adult. The godparent is to prepare for the baptism along with the parents (RBC, #13) and is to be chosen for support rather than for blood relationship. This ministry is no mere ceremonial token, but a long-term rapport with the family and household, carried out in the name of the church itself.

CLERGY

The priest or deacon also serves as a minister of baptism within the "begetting community." The rites lay heavy stress on the priest's duties: the duty, "with the assistance of catechists and other qualified lay people," to prepare the parents and godparents; the duty "to administer baptism"

(GI, #13); the duty to prepare families for baptism and to help them in the further formation; the duty to visit and support the families; the duty to celebrate baptism "with proper dignity . . . adapted to . . . the families . . . with care and devotion" (RBC, #5, 7).

A closer reading, however, provides a diverse and engaging picture of the clergy's role in baptism. To baptize is so central to their ministry, to the life of the church, that even bishops, "as leaders of the entire liturgical life in the church committed to them, . . . should personally celebrate baptism, especially at the Easter Vigil" (GI, #12). This begetting, this bringing forth people of faith, is the real presence of the Risen Christ: "At every celebration of this sacrament they should remember that they act in the church in the name of Christ and by the power of the Holy Spirit." (GI, #11)

The rites describe the priest as a minister of hospitality, extending a welcome to the family before, during and after the baptism: "He must try to be understanding and friendly to all" (RBC, #7). He is also "diligent in the ministry of the word," careful to reveal the living presence of Christ through the word (GI, #11). Similarly, he is a liturgical minister, celebrating the rite "with proper dignity, with care and devotion," dealing pastorally with "the circumstances and wishes of the families involved" (RBC, #7). The priest is likewise a minister of formation, in collaboration with other members of the community. As always, the priest's ministry is that of convener and coordinator of other ministries and ministers.

When the *Rite of Baptism for Children* appeared in 1969, its language was almost radical, calling for the pastor to be friendly in the liturgical celebration; insisting on formation of the adults if the rite were to be authentic; pressing the priest to collaborate with "qualified lay people"; implying that these lay people even could assist in the preparation for baptism, "with appropriate pastoral guidance" from the clergy, of course.

We have traveled many miles since these "radical" words. Twenty-five years later, most of these directives seem mild, even quaint, and rather patronizing. This is an indication of the enormous shifts in self-understanding and in ministry the church has experienced, shifts that give every indication of continuing at full pace. In the typical parish, the ministries that the 1969 rite consigned to the clergy are more frequently the domain of parishioners. These ministries and functions are becoming increasingly decentralized and declericalized.

In parishes large and small, rural and urban, the formation of parents and godparents, the hospitality and pastoral visits and supporting relationships, the reflection on the word and the preaching, the liturgical/musical planning and expertise—all these ministerial roles are carried out by a wide array of "qualified lay people." In many parish communities, these are now primarily ministries of the parish community, not of the parish staff. Not infrequently, the deacon of a parish will preside at many of the community's baptism. The renewal of the rites of initiation is bringing about the renewal of the initiating community.

The ministry of the pastor has everything in common with the other ministries of baptism. His ministry entails a role and a relationship before, during and after the ritual celebration itself. His "pastoring" role is shared with the entire community; his "formation in faith" role parallels that of the parents; his "supporting and witnessing" role echoes the role of the godparent. Baptism is not primarily the priest's responsibility: To baptize is the essence of the entire church in all its parts. The priest's role consists largely of animating the "begetting community" as it goes about its ministry.

Notes

1. Regis Duffy, "My Fellow Beginners," *Christian Initiation Resources*, volume 2, no. 1 (New York: Sadlier, 1981), 1–6.

2. The *Rite of Baptism for Children* and the *Rite of Christian Initiation of Adults* use the term "celebrant" to refer to the minister who leads the community in the celebration of its rites. In this book I often use the term "presider" to refer to this minister and "celebrants" to refer to members of the assembly.

Chapter 2

THE RITE OF BAPTISM

When the church gathers to baptize children, the rite it uses has high standards in mind. For one thing, the *Rite of Baptism for Children* (RBC) presumes the "full, conscious and active participation" of the assembly: "The faithful . . . all . . . take an active part in the rite." (RBC, #32) This is, after all, a liturgy of and by and with the church. It is not a sacrament done to the children, but a sacrament affecting and building up the baptismal faith of the church itself. The baptism of the children is the excuse or occasion around which the church publicly declares its own baptismal faith; the baptismal event happens to the church more than it happens to the children.

So the rite presumes that the community gathered—whether 20 or 1,200 people—is the primary celebrant, fully engaged in the ritual event. The rite even anticipates that the actual baptism, the most revealing and awkward moment of the rite, will occur "within view of the congregation" (RBC, #52), at "a suitable place within the church" so the entire congregation can participate. Using a temporary vessel for the baptismal water and moving the baptism away from the baptistry are justified (GI, #19, 25, 26) if these will allow the entire assembly to participate more fully.

The rite expects the assembly to celebrate the sacrament. This is consistent with the revisions of all sacramental rites since the Second Vatican Council, which defined this as a key principle of our liturgical life:

> Liturgical services are not private functions, but are celebrations belonging to the church. . . . Liturgical services involve the whole body of the church; they manifest it and have effects upon it. . . . Whenever rites . . . make provision for communal celebration involving the presence and active participation of the faithful, it is to be stressed that this way of celebrating them is to be

preferred, as far as possible, to a celebration that is individual and, so to speak, private. (*Constitution on the Sacred Liturgy, #26, 27*)

The rite expects the active engagement of all; this is to be our usual form of sacramental celebration now. But this expectation conflicts with the still common practice of infant baptism: a semi-private event, its celebration unknown to the parish at large, its participants expecting and expected to be more spectators than celebrants.

THE CONTINUUM IS ALWAYS THE SAME

Before 1969, there was no rite that accounted for infants being baptized; there was simply a condensed version of adult baptism, used for the baptism of infants. The ancient process of initiating adults—a gradual process of incorporation, over an extended period of time, in the public forum with the whole community—was unhurried and deliberate. It remained on the books throughout the centuries, appearing even in the *Roman Ritual (Collectio Rituum)* of the early 1960s. But it was there as a relic, for it was never practiced. For all practical purposes it had disappeared. The extended, public process had long ago shriveled to a brief series of convert classes conducted solely by the clergy, culminating in private baptism, first communion at some other time, and a coincidental confirmation later on.

Throughout most of the church's history, infants have been baptized according to the adult ritual. As the ancient process was compacted for use with adult baptism, the condensed version was used with infant baptism as well. The extended, gradual process was there in miniature, the entire process traced in 20 minutes or less. But it remained an adult rite: The infant was addressed as if capable of responding; the godparents of this "little catechumen" figured prominently in the rite; parents and family and larger community were benignly ignored.

Since 1969, the church has had for the first time a rite of baptism accommodated to infants and young children, the *Rite of Baptism for Children*. In this rite, the infant is not expected to respond to questions; the parents and family and larger community are central to the rite, and the godparent has a secondary role in the liturgy.

But even this "new" rite is based upon the adult ritual. The adult process of initiation, now recovered and restored in the *Rite of Christian Initiation of Adults* (RCIA), is still the model for the baptism of infants and young children. That extended public process of adult initiation, in compact form, is detectable in the *Rite of Baptism for Children*.

The *Rite of Christian Initiation of Adults* describes stages through which both those to be initiated and the initiating community are to pass. The initiation begins with hospitality and welcome, first sharing of expectations by both the community and the individuals (the precatechumenate period). It advances to fuller initiation centered upon the encounter with God's word as proclaimed through the lectionary (the catechumenate period). Then both those to be baptized and the community prepare more intensely to celebrate the paschal mystery (the period of purification and enlightenment), culminating in the sacraments of initiation, normally at the Easter Vigil liturgy. Finally, the neophytes and the community support each other and explore their communal life as the eucharistic people (period of mystagogy).

This continuum for adult initiation is the same framework for the initiation of infants and children. The same progression is spelled out in the *Rite of Baptism for Children*:

■ Hospitality, welcome, expectations, initial commitments

- Fuller incorporation, centered on the word

- More intense spiritual preparation

- Celebration of sacrament

- Prayer at the altar (anticipating the sharing in the eucharist, which is delayed for infants)

- Growth into the communal life

The timetables for full initiation vary considerably in our church. For adults, the catechumenate period alone is to last for at least one full year. They always "are to receive baptism, confirmation and eucharist in a single eucharistic celebration."

Then the period of mystagogy is to extend through the entire Easter Season, for one full year (U.S. Statutes for the Catechumenate, #6, 14, 24). Infants, however, are often baptized soon after birth; baptism, confirmation and eucharist typically are separated by several years. From the perspective of the adult rite, the baptism for children is incomplete, and their initiation process fragmented.

Reconciling these different timetables and their various implications is beyond the scope of this book. The purpose here is to note that even by the various and quite different timetables for initiation in our church, the continuum is always the same: from the sign of the cross, to the book of the scriptures, to the waters of baptism, ultimately to the table and the communal life. The baptism of a child is incomplete initiation in and of itself, but even this single rite bears witness to the progression of initiating people into the Body of Christ.

The *Rite of Baptism for Children* is arranged according to this progression:

- Reception of the Children, #32

- Celebration of God's Word, #44

- Celebration of the Sacrament, #53

- Conclusion of the Rite, #67

RECEPTION OF THE CHILDREN, #32–43

The reception of the children is the action of the church, done in four movements:

1) The church gathers.

2) The presider greets everyone, especially parents and godparents.

3) The parents, godparents and church state their intention and commitments.

4) The children are marked with the sign of the cross by presider, parents and godparents.

GATHERING It is not the words that are important in the act of receiving the children and those who accompany them, but the atmosphere of hospitality and welcome. That is why, when the rite is celebrated at Sunday eucharist, the usual greeting and penitential rite are omitted (#29). This is an abrupt beginning to Sunday eucharist, as if to say that the usual routine does not apply: The matter of welcoming takes precedence. The priority of hospitality is also the reason why the rite expects that the church be gathered if baptism is to occur.

Baptism preferably takes place on Sunday, the day of resurrection. It is the day when Christ gathers the church together in prayer, and the church gathered is the minister of baptism into Christ. The rite urges that baptism be celebrated as a communal, corporate, public event by and with the church—not as an individual, selective, private event by and with the family only.

> It should be conferred in a communal celebration for all the recently born children, and in the presence of the faithful, or at least of relatives, friends and neighbors, who are all to take an active part in the rite. (RBC, #32)

Before 1969, the only rite provided was for the baptism of a single child, and it presumed that the church normally would not be present (except for the "more solemn form of baptism . . . which should not be used too frequently"). The current ritual intentionally lists the "Rite of Baptism for Several Children" before the "Rite of Baptism for One Child" and presumes the church present and actively engaged as liturgical minister. Baptism is "the sacrament of the church's faith and of admittance into the people of God" (RBC, #10), not the celebration of a single household alone. The rite presses this point:

> As far as possible, all recently born babies should be baptized at a common celebration on the same day. Except for a good reason, baptism should not be celebrated more than once on the same day in the same church. (GI, #27)

> Baptism . . . should normally be celebrated in the parish church. . . . Except in case of danger of death, baptism should not be celebrated in private houses. (RBC, #10, 12)

The focus is not on the infant being baptized; this is no longer an adequate understanding of baptism. The focus is, instead, on the church actively baptizing, the "begetting community" in the act of begetting, the church that itself becomes the real subject of the baptismal liturgy. In a real sense, it is the church itself that is once again to be baptized; this is the greater understanding of baptism the rite is calling us to. That's why the rite is so insistent that baptism no longer be approached or practiced as a private matter, no longer parceled out one family or one infant at a time. The pastoral practice of some parishes and some pastors still lags behind the rite—not gathering the church in hospitality and welcome, but still holding separate, quasi-private baptisms for each family. Some even baptize four or five different times on the same Sunday afternoon, one family at a time. This strange practice contrasts sharply with what the rite has in mind.

GREETING AND DIALOGUE   The words of the gathering, the greeting, and the dialogue among the parties are to be shaped by the participants: The rite says repeatedly that the presider, parents and godparents will shape the dialogue in their own words (RBC, #36–40). More important than the particular words used is the fact that the participants publicly state their intentions and commitments, publicly claim the event: What is it you seek? Here is what it will mean, here is what it will demand of you. Are you as parents agreeable to this? Will you as godparent stand by these parents?

The reception of the children is parallel to the Rite of Acceptance into the Order of Catechumens, the first ritual in the process of initiation for adults, when "assembling publicly for the first time, the candidates . . . declare their intention to the church and the church . . . accepts them as persons who intend to become its members" (RCIA, #41). In the rite for children, the parents pledge themselves to an extended process of initiation, and the church pledges itself, in the person of the godparent, to support them. The entire assembly might also be asked to pledge itself to support the parents (as in RCIA, #53): "Are all who are gathered here ready to help these parents?"

SIGNING WITH THE CROSS   The pledge of the church culminates in the signing with the cross, the only part of the reception with explicit text and action (#41). The presider, parents, godparents—and perhaps the entire family group—trace the cross on the child's forehead, an action that will be repeated thousands of times in the child's life. This gesture of blessing and claiming is the high point of the reception, the sharing of a "family heirloom." We "claim you for Christ our savior by the sign of his cross," the church declares. "Receive the sign of your new life as catechumens. . . . It is Christ himself who now strengthens you with this sign of his love," the adult rite says (RCIA, #53).

As with most ritual gestures, this signing is not done primarily for the individual child's sake, but for the benefit of the gathered church. It will speak most clearly for the church when it is simple, large, deliberate, unhurried, obvious. This gesture of belonging also becomes a rich source for preaching. The homilist can easily explore the significance of this sign, which we use so often and reflect on so seldom.

The reception and signing replace the usual greeting and entrance rites if the baptism is celebrated at Sunday Mass. The presider might invite the baptismal party to sign the children, and at the same time invite the members of the assembly to trace the cross on their own foreheads or to make the sign of the cross in the usual manner. In this way the presider can link the signing of those to be baptized with the usual Sunday practice of beginning with this sign of Christ's cross. This helps to enhance the signing and to engage the assembly in this untypical opening rite.

PROCESSION   To move everyone from the reception toward the sharing of the word, the rite envisions a procession with accompanying song at this point (RBC, #42). In fact, the rite calls for a procession with accompanying song to begin each of its four stages:

> **1)** to the door or entrance of the church for the reception (#35)

2) to the ambo or seating area for the liturgy of the word (#42)

3) to the baptistry for the baptism (#52)

4) to the altar for the concluding prayers (#67)

The rite obviously wants us to process! It envisions a liturgy that acts out a journey motif, thus echoing the language and experience of the adult rite of initiation:

> The rite of initiation is suited to a *spiritual journey of adults*. . . . *This journey includes* . . . *the steps marking the catechumens' progress, as they pass, so to speak, through another doorway or ascend to the next level.* (RCIA, #5–6; emphasis added)

In the baptism of children,

> the parts of the rite . . . should be celebrated in different areas of the church which . . . suit the size of the congregation and the several stages of the baptismal liturgy. . . . [Even] the parts of the rite customarily performed in the baptistry may be transferred to some other suitable area of the church. (GI, #26)

The practical matter of getting people from one place to another becomes something else in a liturgical context: a procession. And in the liturgy, a procession is always intended as a three-dimensional metaphor for a journey. A procession may involve a representative number, such as in a gospel procession or an entrance procession, or we may enact our life as pilgrims by a procession of the entire assembly—a communion procession, a procession with palms, the procession from the bonfire of the Easter Vigil.

What better suits the celebration of baptism, the beginning of initiation, than to evoke a journey? The rite wants us to process, to experience and visualize and remember that initiation is a spiritual journey passing through doors and moving along the road with the Risen One—from the welcoming cross, into the living word, through the waters of life and death, ultimately toward the table where our eyes will be opened and we will recognize him in the breaking of the bread.

To benefit from this ritual of procession requires that we pay attention to the several stages of the baptismal liturgy, celebrate the different stages at their appropriate settings in the church space, and move people from one stage to the next with accompanying music. In practice, this means:

- The reception of these children (as with adults in the Rite of Acceptance) takes place at the entrance or doorway of the church. At the threshold, we are invited into the church and into the house of the church. Here we will bless ourselves with the waters of baptism for years to come, to remember how God led us into the church through the saving waters.

- The baptismal party moves to the ambo for the sharing of the word, physically and mentally proceeding from the first welcome to the more serious matter of hearing the word. We are led by God into the church to hear the word and to respond.

- The parents with the children, godparents, other members of the assembly and the ministers process from the area of the word to the baptistry or font. The encounter with the word leads us to the sacrament of rebirth. Processing becomes a physical reminder that all must hear the word in order to come to faith.

- The rite concludes with a procession to gather at the altar. By this movement to the altar, we tell ourselves that the waters of baptism point us toward the eucharistic table and the eucharistic people. We physically remind ourselves that baptism is not complete in and of itself: The climax of initiation is eucharist.

Surely there is good material for some liturgical preaching in this. The celebration of baptism in progressive stages, at the proper places within the church, with processing by some or all present, becomes a metaphor of discipleship for us. Such an approach visually preaches to us about the pilgrimage we are on. It teaches us about the progressive character of initiation.

The baptism will still "work" if the baptismal party never moves throughout the rite. It will still "work" if the reception, readings, baptism and anointing, and Lord's Prayer all occur in the same place. It will still "work" if the people do not process or progress through the stages of the rite. But we are interested in a "full, conscious, and active participation," in a rich and evocative celebration, not in minimalism. Loosen up, move around, use some traveling music with the processions, and the rite will begin to speak in new and surprising ways. Otherwise we sell this rite short, we fail to see and understand that we too are on the road, going up to Jerusalem with Jesus walking ahead of us (Mark 10:32).

CELEBRATION OF GOD'S WORD, #44–52

Chapter three of this book, on the liturgy of the word, provides a detailed look at the scripture readings for baptism and closely examines the sharing of the word. At this point, the issue to be discussed is this: The service of the word in the celebration of infant baptism is for the sake of the adult community. While the focus of this celebration is the child, it is into the faith of the adult commuity that this child is received. This faith, as St. Paul noted, comes from hearing. Just as the baptism of an adult is preceded by the many proclamations of scripture heard both by the communmity and the catechumen during the period of the catechumenate and by the readings during the Easter Vigil, so too is the baptism of an infant. The pattern of adult initiation, that catechumens are welcomed into the church in order to hear the word, is followed in the *Rite of Baptism for Children*. The Roman presbyter Hippolytus, writing in the early third century, described a catechumen as one who is admitted in order to hear the word of God:

> Those who come forward for the first time to hear the word shall first . . . be questioned about their reason for coming to the faith. And those who have brought them shall bear witness about them, whether they are capable of hearing the word. . . . Catechumens shall continue to hear the word for three years. (Hippolytus, *Apostolic Tradition*, #15, 16)

It is easy to see in this description the model of the present-day Rite of Acceptance into the Order of Catechumens and of the catechumenate period. Learning to hear the word must go on before the catechumen can be baptized or welcomed to the eucharistic table.

In fact, this is the pattern strictly followed in all the sacramental reforms after Vatican II: We must first encounter the word of God before we celebrate the sacramental rite. We thus reveal an important truth to ourselves: This sacrament, any sacrament, has meaning only as a response to God inviting us to faith. We do not celebrate our initiative in this sacramental rite; we are celebrating God's initiative and our attempt to respond. That's why there is always to be a sharing of the word first, and only then the sacramental action.

FOR THE SAKE OF THE ADULT COMMUNITY The catechumen must become attuned to the word of God before there can be full initiation. Likewise, the adult community must encounter the word of God before it can celebrate baptism for children. The rite is clear that this encountering God's word is an adult affair.

As the church invites catechumens to hear God's word in order to come to faith, so the church now invites the adults to hear God's word so there may be faith and baptism for the children. The children simply are incapable of hearing the word and responding in faith, they "cannot have or profess personal faith" (RBC, #1). The baptism and the rest of their initiation is dependent upon the faith and commitment of the adult believers.

The sharing of the word "is directed toward stirring up the faith of the parents, godparents and congregation, and praying in common for the fruits of baptism" (RBC, #17). This is the guiding principle for the entire word service, and for the entire baptism. The church's own baptismal faith is stirred up and enhanced by its celebration of baptism. The church again practices and again learns the listening and responding of discipleship. This sacrament, any sacrament, is for the assembly more than the individual; this baptism is intended to form the adults in faith more than it is intended to happen to the children. What are the fruits of baptism for which we will pray? That the community doing the baptizing will be built up in its baptismal faith.

For the same reason, the rite is for the sake of the adults' faith. Besides expounding on the readings, the one preaching explores "a deeper understanding of the mystery of baptism" and encourages the adult believers in their baptismal responsibilities (RBC, #45). This is a tall order for what is intended as "a short homily." The essential point of the preaching, whether at the Sunday Mass or at a separate celebration of baptism, is that it *address the faith of the community gathered.* What does this celebration of our faith say about our faith, our identity? How does this baptism affect us? What are the responsibilities we as adults and community assume by daring to baptize someone into

Christ and his church? What is it that Christ is leading us to by means of baptism? How are we being baptized into Christ by this baptism?

After the homily, the rite gets a bit confusing. The liturgy of the word is to continue with:

- intercessions

- litany of the saints

- prayer of exorcism and prebaptismal anointing

- procession to the site of the baptism.

If we consider some of the problems of this arrangement, then we might develop a resolution.

The intercessions follow the homily unless a period of silence or a suitable song has been included (#46). The intercessions listed, #47 and #217–220, are all addressed directly to God, an unfamiliar form. They are not addressed to the assembly as an invitation to prayer; they do not end with the standard call to prayer; and so they do not readily elicit a familiar response from the assembly. They are all focused on the baptism and the initiation; but after these specific ones, the regular *general* "petitions are added for the universal church and the needs of the world" (RBC, #29). For this litany to work, the assembly would need a more standard form and invitation to response.

The litany of intercessions "always concludes with the invocation of the saints" (RBC, #216). This litany may accompany the procession with the children, if they were taken out for the liturgy of the word (#48), although this is seldom done in U.S. parishes.

In the initiation of adults (RCIA, #219), this litany fulfills its traditional role of accompanying the procession to the baptistry or place of baptism. This may be worth consider-ing with the baptism of children as well. It is much more common for all to process to the place of baptism than for the children to reenter the assembly in procession. Besides, it is simply awkward to have two litanies with different responses take place back to back, as the rite provides. Such an arrangement does not work in practice.

The prayer of exorcism and the prebaptismal anointing parallel the three minor rites of the catechumenate—the minor exorcisms, blessings and anointings (RCIA, #81– 103)—and they contain elements from each. The prayer is "drawn up in the style of an exorcism" (like the minor exorcisms) and leads into "either the anointing with the oil of catechumens [like the anointings] or the laying on of hands [like the blessings]" (RBC, #17). The rite indicates that the anointing is seldom to be omitted, which means the laying on of hands is seldom to be used (#51). In the adult rite the three minor rites express different meanings, helping to clarify the dynamics of initiation (exorcisms, RCIA, #90), to provide courage and peace along the catechumens' way (blessings, #95) and strengthen them in their quest for faith (anointings, #99). In the baptism of children, these ritual gestures, words and meanings are blended together and are rather unclear. Is exorcism, strengthening as for a catechumen, or blessing and laying on of hands to predominate?

The procession to the place of baptism follows. Where will the baptism occur? The rite suggests three different arrangements:

■ a baptistry separated from the church and assembly, to which all process

■ a baptistry visible by the congregation, to which the baptismal party alone processes

■ a baptism "celebrated in a suitable place within the church" for the sake of the assembly's participation, to which only the parents and godparents bring the child.

In all cases, the rite presumes that the baptism is visible to the assembly and that the assembly is actively present. It also presumes a procession to the waters, accompanied in typical fashion with "an appropriate song, e.g., Psalm 23" (RBC, #52). But in the typical parish in the United States, the baptistry is not distant, the procession neither long nor all-inclusive, and accompanying music nearly nonexistent.

Among these three elements—intercessions, the exorcism and the anointing —which are the more important? What needs to be highlighted or diminished? How might this part of the rite be best celebrated? The order would include:

1) *The general intercessions.* These should be prayed in a typical Sunday pattern and form. If some of the suggested intercessions are used, they should be rewritten to address the assembly as invitations to pray. General prayers are offered first: for the world, for the church, for those in need. Prayers more particular to the baptismal gathering, this liturgy, are then offered: for the families, for the local parish, for the parents.

2) *The prayer of exorcism.* This is meant as a short (and minor) prayer for strengthening. "We pray for these children" is the heart of this prayer. This can be strengthened, legitimately, by inviting the members of the baptismal party to place a hand in prayer upon the children or infants to be baptized.

3) *The anointing with the oil of catechumens.* This is a minor, optional rite with adult catechumens. In baptism for children, this anointing (like the preceding prayer of exorcism) marks a transition and conclusion to the liturgy of the word.

Both the prayer of exorcism and the anointing should be completed before anyone proceeds toward the font, that is, while the baptismal party is with the congregation at Sunday Mass, or before the baptismal party moves to the font, if at a separate celebration of baptism. At a smaller

gathering, the party could stand for the intercessions, then encircle the children and parents for the prayer of exorcism (during which all place a hand on the children) and the anointing.

In practice, these two elements (the exorcism prayer and the anointing) seem obscure, their meanings rather unclear to people. In the lengthy process of adult initiation, the three minor rites can be differentiated from each other and provide separate, complementary meanings. But in the compact rite of baptizing children, these minor rites have been amalgamated into two elements with muddled meanings. Perhaps in the context of the *Rite of Baptism for Children* it helps to see these elements as conclusions to the intercessions—prayer by word and gesture for the strength and guidance these children will need. They are minor, transitional elements to draw our "praying in common for the fruits of baptism" to a close.

4) *The procession, with the litany of the saints.* The procession marks a clear and decisive shift to a different set of rites about to begin at the water. The procession says to everyone—even if everyone is not processing— that something important is finished now and something else, also important, is about to begin. The procession benefits the entire assembly, drawing them to the waters.

It works well to use the litany of the saints as music with this procession, no matter how long or how short it is. With or without a cantor, with or without accompaniment, people easily join in the litany. We invoke our ancestors in faith as we move toward the waters, to accompany us on this journey we make.

We will not resolve here the issue of placement of the baptismal font in the worship space. But regardless of where the font or temporary vessel is placed, the rite anticipates that some people process at this point, that they process somewhere, and that they then get out of the way.

The rite anticipates that the entire assembly will be visually engaged with the rites at the font. This is no small consideration in construction or renovation of our worship spaces, and it is a major change from our former practices. Even the *Rite of Christian Initiation of Adults* (#218 and 219) presses the point that the assembly must be able to see what is going on with baptism; the font or temporary vessel of water and the placement of people must be done "in such a way as not to block the view of the congregation."

CELEBRATION OF BAPTISM, #53–66

The actual celebration of the sacrament takes place in many stages: the blessing and invocation of God over the baptismal water, renunciation of sin and profession of faith, anointing with chrism, clothing with white garment, the presentation of the lighted candle and the ephphetha, or prayers over the ears and mouth.

BLESSING AND INVOCATION OVER THE WATERS. In this progressive rite, we approach the third station, the font. Once the baptismal party is gathered there and the assembly is able to see and hear, the presider says a word to gather everyone, to the effect of "Now we ask God's blessing and action." The presider then pronounces the remarkable prayer (#54), using one of three forms provided.

The prayer is usually referred to as a blessing of the water, but that's not really a good description. It is clearly a prayer blessing God, formally called "Blessing and Invocation of God over Baptismal Water." This blessing follows the same pattern as the eucharistic prayer of the Mass, and it is a eucharistic—giving thanks—prayer in the fullest sense.

> ■ *We give thanks and remember.* We give thanks and praise to God by recounting the saving history and events that prompt the thanks and praise.

In a sense, we remind God of all that God has done in the past.

■ *We make petition.* We ask God to continue that legacy of saving action. We ask God to be consistent, to act decisively now as in the past. We remind God that the church is now the heir to the entire tradition, which stretches back to "the very dawn of creation."

■ *We invoke the presence and action of God's Spirit.* This epiclesis, or invocation of the Spirit, is the high point of any eucharistic prayer. Act now, we say to God, "by the power of the Spirit." And we tell God what it is we want the Spirit to do: to raise those who pass through the waters, like you raised Christ.

■ *We close with another blessing of God,* expressed in some standard form. The closing doxology here is short, compared to the longer one at Mass ("through him, with him . . . all glory and honor is yours . . .").

Here is the same pattern of "giving thanks, remembering, petitioning and praising" that characterizes our other eucharistic prayers. But notice that the prayer is not a blessing *of* the water, not a preparation *of* the water, not a dedication *of* the water. It is, rather, a prayer seeking God's action consistent with what has happened in the recited history. It is a prayer that God bless and animate what we do here, that God act through what we do.

If the prayer is addressed to God, it is also directed to the praying community. See what we tell ourselves by this prayer. By reminding God of the saving history that has involved water, we remind ourselves of the significance this rite with water carries. By asking God to act through this baptism, we tell ourselves what this baptism will mean. We tell ourselves by this prayer that God is indeed acting through our baptismal rite.[1]

So the blessing of God is addressed to God, and it is also expressing to the praying community the meaning of what we do at the font. Hence the rite insists that the blessing prayer is always to be proclaimed, to "clearly express the mystery of salvation which the church recalls and proclaims" (GI, #21). No more is the water blessed once at Easter and used for an entire year, as was the old practice. Now the water is to be clean, and the font or temporary vessel "should be very clean and attractive" (GI, #18, 19). The blessing is for the sake of the assembly celebrating baptism, not for the sake of the water. So the giving thanks and remembering and confident petitioning of God is to be done every time we gather at the font, that the blessing prayer will renew us (RBC, #55).

The first form of the blessing prayer is from the Easter Vigil liturgy. The second form is in responsorial fashion, using first an acclamation and then an invocation by the assembly ("Blessed be God" and "Hear us, Lord" are suggested). The third form is also in responsorial fashion, with an acclamation by the assembly in the first part (the "praise" part) of the prayer. The sacramentary proposes this blessing prayer be sung at the Easter Vigil; there are good musical arrangements of the prayer available. When the baptism of children is celebrated at Sunday Mass, it would be fitting to use the same musical arrangement of the prayer as the parish uses at the Easter Vigil. The second and third forms of the prayer could be recited by the presider with an acclamation sung by the assembly; again, the parish's Easter Vigil or Easter Season music would be an appropriate source for this acclamation.

Remember that this prayer, indeed the entire baptism, is for the benefit of the assembly, a proclamation of faith to the assembly. No wonder the rite says the assembly must be able to see and hear what goes on at the font! What will enhance that active engagement? Singing the text of the blessing? Using the responsorial form of the prayer with sung responses by all? Pouring pitchers of water into the temporary container throughout the blessing prayer? Lifting handfuls of water, stirring the waters, during the reciting of the saving history? Stirring the waters at the invocation of the Spirit? The blessing and invocation of God over the baptismal water need not be dramatic, but it does need more than the perfunctory recitation of a text.

RENUNCIATION OF SIN, PROFESSION OF FAITH

After the blessing, the adults are called upon to restate the beliefs that give the rite its meaning. They do so in the name of the whole church and for the sake of the children. They renew their baptismal vows, publicly turning from evil and turning toward faith. In ancient times, the candidates would literally turn—facing the west, the place of darkness, for the renunciation and sin, then turning toward the east, the direction of the rising sun and of Christ's return, to profess the baptismal faith. This ritual renunciation and profession is at the heart of all initiation and discipleship. It is the baptismal business to which we all return every year at Lent, called on Ash Wednesday to turn away from sin and at the Easter Vigil to renew our vows.

The rite provides two forms for the renunciation of sin, the first with more traditional language ("Satan, his works, his promises") and the second "a fuller one using a contemporary vocabulary that is more intelligible to people today"[2]—"Do you reject sin, so as to live in the freedom of God's children?" The profession of faith is then made in the traditional threefold pattern, the same credal language used at all baptisms and by the whole church at the Easter liturgies.

This renunciation of sin and profession of faith by parents and godparents is to be endorsed by the presider and assembly, by some simple declaration or by a "suitable song"

(RBC, #59). The profession of faith by the parents and godparents is thus acknowledged and affirmed. But in practice, this dialogue seems too weak; the intended interaction does not work well. If the baptism is celebrated at Sunday Mass, the voices of the baptismal party seem too few and too weak, and the response by presider and assembly is likewise awkward or feeble.

One alternative is to have the entire assembly join the parents and godparents in the renunciation and profession. Everyone present responds as one voice, collectively "turning from sin" and "turning toward faith." When baptism occurs at Sunday Mass the creed is omitted, "since the profession of faith by the entire community before baptism takes its place" (RBC, #29). In lieu of the dialogue form that the rite proposes, the presider invites the assembly to repeat its Easter/baptismal vows together. The assembly's involvement reiterates that this faith professed is "not the private possession of the individual family" (RBC, #4). The dialogue form the rite proposes is not as important as the fact that evil is renounced and faith is professed by those seeking baptism.

BAPTISM The presider then calls forth each baptismal party in turn by asking the parents and godparents their intentions one final time. He then baptizes the child with the trinitarian formula, immersing or pouring water over the child with each of the three phrases.

We must make note of proper and improper roles in the act of baptizing. The *minister of the church* does the baptizing, taking the child for the immersion or else pouring water over the child, whom the parents hold. The *parents* present the child to the church for the immersion itself, then receive the child out of the immersion font. Or they hold the child for the pouring of water by the presider. In other words, *the church in the person of its minister does the baptizing*, not the individual family or the parents. The parents present the child to be baptized by the church into the faith, which "is not the private possession of the individual family." The child is baptized by the church, a ritual image that one is baptized into something greater than oneself or one's own family. It is simply not appropriate for the parents to bring the child to the water and themselves immerse the child, no matter how friendly or gracious or pastoral this seems. The family does not baptize, the church does. It is for this same reason that the rite insists baptism be celebrated at the church, not in the family's home (RBC, #10, 12).

Finally, *the godparents* have a secondary role at this moment of baptism, a striking change from the former rite. Godparents used to present the child, a consequence of using the adult rite (with the godparent accompanying the adult catechumen to the font) for the baptism of infants. Parents were relegated to insignificance with the old rite; the mother often was not even present for the baptism. The current rite corrects that imbalance, stressing that "parents have a more important ministry and role in the baptism than the godparents. . . . The parents should be present in the celebration. . . . They (and especially the mother) carry the child to the font" (RBC, #5). This "new" practice caused quite a stir when the 1969 rite was first used. Twenty-five years later, the secondary role for godparents is not a significant pastoral issue. It has been replaced by other "new" issues.

The method for baptism, whether of adults or children, is one such issue. If we look at the ritual texts themselves, it is obvious that the revised rites for baptism strongly prefer immersion as the proper sacramental method. The texts have grown more insistent about this since the *Rite of Baptism for Children* was published in 1969. But if we look at pastoral practice, we find this preferred method very slow to be implemented or widely encouraged, continuing to meet strong reaction and opposition.

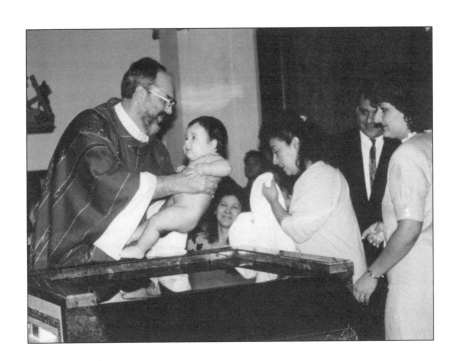

In 1969, the texts reintroduced this ancient practice, saying it was now as "legal" as the familiar infusion (pouring water over the forehead). They even called immersion "more suitable as a symbol of participation in the death and resurrection of Christ" than pouring water over the forehead (GI, #22). By the final time the text of the *Rite of Christian Initiation of Adults* was published with the adaptations for the United States in 1988, the advantage of immersion as the sacramental sign was more explicitly spelled out:

> Therefore in the celebration of baptism *the washing with water should take on its full importance as the sign of that mystical sharing in Christ's death and resurrection* through which those who believe in his name die to sin and rise to eternal life. *Either immersion or the pouring of water should be chosen . . . to ensure the clear understanding that this washing is not a mere purification rite but the sacrament of being joined to Christ.*

> The celebrant baptizes each candidate either by immersion, option A, or by the pouring of water, option B. . . . If baptism is by immersion, of the whole body or of the head only, decency and decorum should be preserved. . . . The celebrant, immersing the candidate's whole body or head three times, baptizes the candidate in the name of the Trinity. (RCIA, #213, 226, emphasis added)

> *Baptism by immersion is the fuller and more expressive sign of the sacrament, and therefore is preferred. Although it is not yet a common practice in the U.S., provision should be made for its more frequent use in the baptism of adults.* At the least, the provision of the RCIA for partial immersion, namely, immersion of the candidate's head, should be taken into account. (U.S. Statutes for the Catechumenate, #17, emphasis added)

"Baptism is not a mere purification rite but the sacrament of being joined to Christ"; this has special import for us when it comes to infant baptism. We are growing out of the paltry liturgical practice and the picayune sacramental understanding that reinforced each other. That infant baptism was indeed a purification rite, a ritual rinsing away of original sin, was all the meaning we looked for and all the meaning we found in a minimalist, minuscule pouring. Baptism washes away original sin, the ritual practice said to us, and that's precisely what we believed.

But the church itself is calling us to a more traditional and richer *practice* of baptism, and so is calling us to a more traditional and richer *understanding* of baptism. The liturgical principle is true: How we *practice* baptism expresses and shapes how we *understand* baptism. And it is obvious by now that this rite of the church is challenging us to some "new" and more authentic practices and perspectives on baptism.

It is amazing how this liturgical and pastoral reform has been avoided. In the diocese of Des Moines, for instance, 25 years after the church's endorsement of baptism by immersion, only three of ninety parishes have fonts suitable for immersion of adults and infants. This reform in baptismal practice has been equally slow in other dioceses. There are even parishes with state-of-the-art fonts that nonetheless refuse to practice immersion.

There are all sorts of reasons why baptism of infants by immersion "won't work" or "isn't preferable." But we should instead keep an eye on why it *will* work, how it *is* feasible, why it *is* preferable. People will not understand baptism for children in new ways—as new birth or as coming from the womb or as passing from death into life —until we start experiencing baptism in new ways.

Baptizing infants by full, naked immersion is guaranteed to get an assembly's attention. When was the last time parishioners ever were stirred by a central ritual action?

When we immerse infants, people will remember the actual baptism as the most provocative part! That itself is desirable—participants leaving a sacramental rite, pondering what the ritual means. Thus begin the questions and the reflections and the new understandings.

How to baptize by immersion?

■ Discuss this in advance with parents and parish community, assure them the child will not catch pneumonia or drown, explain why the church is calling for the return of this practice. Remind people that the Orthodox church has been immersing infants for 1500 years and has yet to lose a single one to a baptismal mishap.

■ If the font is not suited to immersion (most older fonts are not), arrange for a temporary vessel large enough to hold sufficient water.

■ Heat the water in the font "if the climate requires" (GI, #20), or put warm water in the temporary vessel. If water is added to the vessel at the "Blessing and Invocation of God over the Baptismal Water," use a pitcher of hot water to ensure a warm temperature for the immersion.

■ Be sure the presider has practiced. This will help to assure the presider that he can hold a wet baby safely and securely, and to realize that the child will survive and even enjoy the immersion (especially if the water is warm).

■ Suggest that the child be brought to the baptism wrapped in a blanket and wearing only a diaper, which is removed just before the immersion.

■ If the temporary vessel is long enough, the presider holds the baby in both hands and lowers the infant into the water. If the vessel is too short for this, the baby is lowered feet first into the water, or can be seated in the water while water is poured over his or her head.

■ The parents take the baby in a towel to warm and dry the infant for the anointing and dressing to come.

If immersion is unfeasible at this time, then do the next option: pouring water over the child's head. But remember that this, too, always needs to be full, evocative, simple, visible, audible. No pristine trickles on a baby's forehead are allowed at Catholic baptisms anymore. This water bath, this passing through the waters, symbolizes our death and rebirth; no tidy spoonful of water can do justice to this great mystery.

Some presiders hold the baby up for all to see after the baptism. This caught on after the television mini-series "Roots," in which one of the characters held his newborn son up in a gesture of thanksgiving. But it's a strange gesture to add to a Christian baptism. Why do some latch on to it? Partly because the rituals we already have are so poorly and feebly practiced. The real gestures of presentation, the real ritual actions that should rivet people's attention and grab the assembly's imagination, are the action of baptizing and the action of anointing. The gesture borrowed from a made-for-TV movie creeps in because we're not doing justice to the powerful gestures that are already part of the rite. An assembly that experiences the robust celebration of its own rites would have no need to import gestures.

The late Eugene Walsh used to say that the better we do the sacramental sign, the more loudly God speaks through it. So for the sake of the great mystery to be revealed by our sacramental sign, pour water. Pour plenty of water, handfuls of water, pour a pitcher of water. Get the baby wet, get the font and floor wet, get the alb wet, get the blanket wet. Life and death are represented here, drowning and divine rescue are represented here, bursting forth from the waters of chaos and creation are represented here, the waters of birth are represented here. Never mind neat and tidy; the greater concern is that this central ritual be a worthy symbol of what it represents.

ANOINTING WITH CHRISM   Immediately after the immersion or pouring of water is completed, the baptized children are anointed with the chrism. The presider makes a declaration over those to be anointed (RBC, #62), the text coming from the former rite of baptism. God now anoints you, it says, by means of our anointing you. God anoints you to conform you to Christ the Anointed One.

This is clearly a "Christ" anointing, a "priest, prophet and king" anointing, a "living body of Christ" anointing. This is the royal anointing derived from Israel's history, where priest, prophet and king were anointed and so marked for office and service. This regal anointing has been a part of Christian baptism since at least the second century. It is different from the "strengthening" anointing before baptism, different from the "spirit" anointing later with confirmation. This, instead, is the "becoming like Christ the Anointed One" anointing, where we reveal who this child now is and to whom this newborn disciple now belongs.

Before baptism, we anointed the child on the breast to symbolize strengthening. Later, in confirmation, we anoint on the forehead with the laying on of hands to symbolize the legacy of the Spirit. But now we crown the child on the *top of the head*, on the whole of the person, to symbolize this one becoming like Christ. This regal anointing is on "the crown of the head." This is now a royal child, a priestly, royal, prophetic child, part of the Anointed One. This anointing, the rite says, "signifies the royal priesthood of the baptized and enrollment in the fellowship of God's people" (RBC, #18). To do justice to the sign, we need:

■ *Chrism.* This, in contrast to the other oils of our liturgical life, is scented, perfumed. We need plenty of chrism for use with initiations throughout the year. We need chrism that is heavily and pleasantly scented, so we and everyone around it know at once this is the "Christ" oil. Be sure the parish gets all the chrism it needs from the diocese, and be sure this supply is sweet-smelling and pleasing. Add your own oil-based perfume to the oil if necessary. The bishop alone consecrates the chrism for use in the diocese, but the parish must ensure the supply and scent are adequate.

■ *Container.* The chrism requires a suitable container that itself is attractive and appealing. This oil deserves a cut glass or crystal or other fine container that literally can be enshrined by the font throughout the year. At the baptismal anointing, the chrism can be poured directly from this large container onto the head, or some can be poured into a smaller glass cup or dish for use with the anointing. A metal thimble filled with gooey cotton and rancid chrism, hidden in a sacristy drawer until required, simply won't do anymore.

■ *A full anointing.* The chrismation is meant to reveal God transforming all who are anointed. This anointing is not for the baby's sake but for the church's sake. It is not *to the infant* that God speaks through our anointing, but *to the church* that God speaks through our anointing. The better the anointing, the more loudly God speaks *to the church* about belonging to Christ. Oil is to be poured out on each child's head and rubbed in. The whole top of the head is to be rubbed with the scented Chrism. This is to be a lavish anointing, not a miserly afterthought. The oil is poured out and rubbed in; a dab of oil on the presider's thumb, smudged on the forehead (as is often done) and then wiped off doesn't even come close.

Oil is intended to stain and soak into what it touches; this regal oil is intended to stain and perfume and brand the child, so everyone knows this is a royal child. This anointing can be messy. But if the child is still naked after the immersion or pouring, wrapped in a blanket or towel only, then no one need worry about tidiness. Warn the families ahead of time that the infant's head is to be rubbed with oil, and suggest they leave the bonnet at home.

CLOTHING WITH A WHITE GARMENT   The rites that follow the baptismal washing and anointing reiterate the meanings of what has happened and "give expression to the effects of the sacrament" (RCIA, #214). These lesser rites utilize some of the earliest Christian reflections, or *mystagogia*, upon the baptismal rituals.

St. Paul asked, What does dropping your old clothes, being baptized naked, and putting on new garments mean? It means you "drop" the old distinctions and prejudices, and now you "put on Christ." Let your new garments indicate you are "clothing yourself" with new ways of living (see Galatians 3:27–28 or Colossians 3:9–13). The rite picks up this Pauline language as the child is dressed in a baptismal garment. This putting on of new robes is intended as the clothing of an unclothed child. In other words, "it is desirable that the families provide the garment" (RBC, #63), and that the family christening gown or baptismal robe now be put on the child for the first time. This rite makes sense when the unclothed child is immersed, remains naked and is clothed in celebration as a sign of now being "clothed in Christ." It takes only a moment to put a diaper and a new gown on the child, and the rite provides a theological reflection for this ancient, pragmatic step; as Paul would say, You were naked, were baptized, now you put on a new robe, and this is what it means.

This minor rite limps badly if the child is baptized while fully clothed, already wearing the baptismal finery. The weakness is only compounded when a parish lays an embroidered cloth or bib or "baby stole" over the fully robed child and says, *This* is your baptismal robe. Worse, some parishes simply use a purificator, laying it on the fully clothed child, thus saying, Pretend this liturgical napkin is your baptismal robe; act as if it is the sign of your new dignity. And then, of course, the purificator is snatched back. What is going on here?

The problem is not that the parish lacks a good bib-maker; this garment is not meant to come from the parish or be bought through a catalog. The problem is that we cheapen our rituals and then try to cover our tracks. The problem is that we avoid immersion and naked babies like the plague, then wonder why this minor dressing rite makes no sense. Even Catholic babies are born naked. It's okay for them to be naked once in awhile. They can even be naked in church; that's allowed now.

It bears repeating: The church, the assembly, has a right to the robust celebration of its own rites. If we take full immersion baptism seriously, then dressing the naked child in a fine baptismal robe will make sense and will help reveal what baptism means: We are "putting on Christ" like new clothes. Otherwise, skip the garment rite. This minor rite is a metaphor playing on a transformation —undressed before, dressed now—to open up the meaning of the baptismal transformation. If the one transformation is not clear, the metaphor stumbles, and the meaning of the other transformation is obscured. Don't compound the problem by pretending to clothe a fully clothed child while saying how significant this pretending is.

LIGHTED CANDLE The rite of lighting the candle likewise is intended to shed light upon the significance of the baptism: "The presentation of a lighted candle shows that they are called to walk as befits the children of light"

(RCIA, #214). This rite makes sense if the newly baptized are adults; it survives in this rite for infants, nuanced as a reminder to the adult believers of their responsibilities.

The rite and the directive given by the presider again borrow language and imagery from early Christianity. The Gospel of John and various epistles play with the imagery of darkness and light to explain Christ: "In him was life, and the life was the light of all people. The light shines in the darkness, and the darkness did not overcome it." (John 1:4–5) They use it as well to explore the baptismal transformation: "For you are all children of light and children of the day; we are not of the night or of darkness" (1 Thessalonians 5:5); "Whoever says, 'I am in the light,' while hating a brother or sister, is still in the darkness." (1 John 2:9)

But in practice, it must be said that this rite does not work well. The presider is to hold the Easter candle, presenting this light to the newly baptized. Then a parent or godparent is to light a smaller candle from the flame, while the presider declares to the adults what this means: "This light is entrusted to you to be kept burning brightly. These children have been enlightened by Christ."

The metaphorical language is obvious, the parallels clear, but this rite in the context of infant baptism is awkward and overstated. The Easter candle is not easily moved or held by the presider, who typically gestures toward the candle or only refers to it. The baptismal candle is sometimes hard to light from the larger candle; people are often unsure who is to light the baptismal candle, who is to receive it and hold it. Besides, how long is it appropriate for the candle to burn? Through the rest of Sunday Mass? Until the presentation of gifts? Until the closing rite at the altar, if this is a smaller celebration of baptism (#67 indicates the lighted candles are carried to the altar for the closing)? The declaration by the presider is too long for what is a very short action. The action does not bear up well with this declaration, which is even longer than that found with the anointing.

This minor candle rite needs to be simplified. The presider might invite one of the parents to light a candle from the Easter candle, and say:

> To the children: N. and N., you are the light of the world. Receive the light of Christ into your life.

> To the adults and assembly: May we help these children to walk always as people of the light.

EPHPHETHA, OR PRAYER OVER EARS AND MOUTH

The last element with the baptism rite is seldom used. The ephphetha rite parallels the healing story in Mark 7, when Jesus freed the man who had hearing and speech impediments. In the old baptismal practice, this rite was the last exorcism, done at the entrance of the baptistry just before the renunciation of sin. The priest closely followed the gospel account: He took saliva on his thumb and touched this to the ears of the adult or infant ("Ephphetha, which means 'Be opened!'") and then to the nostrils ("So that you may perceive the fragrance of God's sweetness. But you, O devil, depart; for the judgment of God has come."). In our present baptismal rituals, the exorcistic character of the ephphetha has been dropped, as has the use of saliva. In the initiation of adults, this rite remains as an option for use on Holy Saturday, a minor rite to "impress on the elect their need of grace in order that they may hear the word of God and profess it for their salvation" (RCIA, #197).

But in the *Rite of Baptism for Children*, the ephphetha is the final explanatory rite following baptism. Here it is given a future twist, a prayer that Christ "may soon touch your ears to receive his word, and your mouth to proclaim his faith" (RBC, #65).

How does this rite "explain" baptism or aid our understanding of baptism's significance? It does not play with transformation imagery, as the dressing rite and the candle rite do. It does attempt to use metaphorical language— Christ touches your ears and your mouth by means of our touching your ears and mouth. According to Bugnini, it is meant to reveal that baptism empowers us "to hear the word of God, to open their mouths in praise of the Lord, and to take an active part in the liturgical assembly and the life of the church."[3]

But even he acknowledges that in the preparation of this new rite "there was a lively discussion about whether or not to keep this rite. The experts disagreed." Its inclusion was very tentative: It would be used "if the conference of bishops decides to preserve it. In the United States, it may be performed at the discretion of the minister" (RBC, #65). In pastoral practice, it rarely appears; if the baptism is celebrated at Sunday Mass, it almost always is omitted. Its intended meaning is valuable and edifying, but the rite really does not yield its intended meaning. The metaphor stumbles; the gestures are too foreign to our culture and the scriptural allusions too obscure.

CONCLUSION OF THE RITE, #67–71

On paper, the conclusion seems to be the simplest and easiest part of the baptismal celebration. The baptismal party processes to the altar or sanctuary, allusion is made to the children's future sharing in the eucharist with the assembly, the Lord's Prayer is recited by all, those gathered are blessed and then depart. It seems very pragmatic: Bring the liturgy to a swift and simple close. But we soon find it is also theologically astute: Conclude the baptism of these children by leading them to the table of the eucharist. A closer look will help us celebrate this part of the rite well.

On a practical level, the conclusion will vary according to the setting of the baptism. It requires a little planning, selection of appropriate texts, and some logistical considerations. But it is predictable enough to be handled easily.

AT A SMALL CELEBRATION   If the baptism is celebrated with a smaller gathering and apart from Mass, then the rite intends for the baptismal party once again to process. The people move from the site of the font or the temporary vessel, thus physically and mentally shifting from the font to the altar. The baptismal party can be gathered at the foot of the altar ("Next there is a procession to the altar. . . . The celebrant stands in front of the altar and addresses them," #67–68), or can just as easily be brought forward to encircle the altar. There the Lord's Prayer is introduced and recited by all, as always when we gather there for eucharist. It seems very appropriate to include the sign of peace at this point, especially with a smaller group. In fact, the parents can be invited to bring the child to each member of the baptismal party, for each to bless the newly baptized with peace and with a kiss. Then the presider asks God's blessing on the parents, children and all present. It is fitting for everyone in the baptismal party to lay a hand on the parents or child for this blessing —a physical blessing along with the words. The rite concludes as it began, tracing the sign of the cross, this time on oneself. To close, all may join in a hymn or acclamation.

AT SUNDAY MASS   If the baptism is celebrated at Sunday Mass, much of this conclusion is assumed in the normal Sunday routine. The baptism completed, the baptismal party rejoins the assembly, and the liturgy of the eucharist begins at once. At this parish celebration of initiation, members of the baptismal party would take part in the preparation of the altar and presentation of the gifts.

During the eucharistic prayer, those baptized at Mass are explicitly prayed for, even mentioned by name. These special inserts are listed in the sacramentary, in the "Ritual Masses" section. (See "I. Christian Initiation, #3, Baptism.") There is an insert provided for eucharistic prayers I–IV. In fact, two sets of presidential prayers are provided here and may be used when baptism is celebrated at Mass in place of the standard Sunday prayers.

There is no special procession to the altar or sanctuary for the Lord's Prayer, but the presider nonetheless speaks "of the future reception of the eucharist by the baptized children" (RBC, #19), freely adapting the text provided (#68). At this eucharist all should be invited to receive communion from the cup, if this is not already standard parish practice.

For the final blessing, the presider can invite the families of the newly baptized to step forward and the entire assembly to extend hands in blessing over the parents, godparents and children. The text for the blessing at this Mass is taken from the *Rite of Baptism for Children* (#70). The families might be included in the recessional, and the assembly might be invited to greet them at the church doors.

SIGNIFICANCE OF THE CLOSING RITES   The closing rite is rich in theological significance. The former rite for infant baptism abruptly ended at the font, with the minor rites (the clothing with the baptismal garment, the giving of a lighted candle) and a dismissal. By contrast, the *Rite of Baptism for Children* lays out a different practice and therefore a different understanding of baptism. Baptism does not end with the font; the rite is explicit about this. Baptism, it says, ends in the eucharist.

The members of the baptismal party process toward the altar (unless they are already in the sanctuary because a temporary vessel was used for the baptism). In other words, the adults deliberately shift their focus from font to altar as they physically move from one to the other. Their progression is to remind us of the entire church's journey of discipleship: from the welcoming cross, through the living word, toward the living waters, thus to the table where the living body of Christ always gathers. The baptismal passage and the "Christ-like" anointing are the gateway to the eucharistic table and the eucharistic community. We know now, from the fuller context of initiation and from our rediscovered experience with adult initiation, that baptism is not complete in and of itself. It is completed and fulfilled by coming into the eucharist.

> From the baptistry, the newly baptized children are carried in procession to the altar. The point of this rite is to foreshadow the completion of Christian initiation by confirmation and the eucharist. The celebrant reminds the parents of this before all join in reciting the Our Father.[4]

That was the intent of the reformers, anyway. The group physically moves to the altar, where explicit reference is made to our regular gathering here and the children's future sharing in the eucharist here. Even if the baptism occurs at Sunday Mass, the presider situates baptism in the context of full initiation at this point, reminding everyone that baptism begins the journey and does not end it. Then all join in the Lord's Prayer, praying as we always do when we gather at table with the Risen Christ and one another.

The conclusion thus sheds light upon the meaning and significance of baptism, in its own concrete and simple way. This is done for the benefit of the church, not the children, for the edification of the adults around the child and of the entire assembly. The conclusion is a faint echo of confirmation and the sharing in the eucharist, which are delayed for these children. But they are an immediate reminder to the adult church that baptism means coming into the community that breaks bread here and recognizes Christ shared here.

Especially if the baptism occurs at Sunday Mass, the sharing of communion, which now follows, reminds the assembly of that same reality. That, in fact, is the rationale used for the practice of baptizing at Sunday Mass: "So that the entire community may be present *and the necessary relationship between baptism and eucharist may be clearly seen*" (RBC, #9; emphasis added). Even if baptism is celebrated at another time and with a smaller gathering, the explicit movement to the altar and the explicit reference to the eucharist are to occur. "The point of this rite is to foreshadow the completion of Christian initiation."

Would it not be better—a more explicit statement, more traditional, and more consistent with the other rites of initiation—if the children were confirmed and given the eucharist *at this same liturgy?* Why this mere *echo* of confirmation and eucharist, which are actually refused the children for years to come? Doing justice to these questions would require another work entirely. There is no shortage of materials on the market now, calling us to examine these pastoral and sacramental questions. We cannot adequately address or resolve these questions here, but we must recognize them as insightful and legitimate questions. They are new questions and alternative perspectives that have been brought out in the open by our changing baptismal rites and practices.

These important questions have been raised precisely by the changed baptismal rites for both adults and children. Our changing experience of baptism and full initiation is leading us into new understandings of baptism and full initiation. And these different understandings of initiation are, indeed, raising even further questions for us. One generation ago, ending the children's baptism at the font was sufficient. Today, immersing the children, engaging the assembly as the true subject and primary minister of baptism, and ending the baptismal celebration by appeal to eucharist is to be the norm. Tomorrow, this richer pastoral

practice may have convinced us that an allusion to full (but delayed) initiation no longer will suffice.

But this discussion is useless if the conclusion of the rite is not properly or adequately celebrated. In pastoral practice, it often is misunderstood and botched. It is no longer adequate simply to wrap up baptism at the side of the font with an Our Father said by everyone, as if the Lord's Prayer were tacked on to the old rite for no apparent reason. It is inappropriate to skip a procession and a gathering around the altar as if these details of the rite were gimmicks or too much bother. It is poor celebration if we fail to tie this baptism to our parish's altar and weekly eucharistic meal, as if our approach to baptism hasn't changed a bit in the last 30 years. The church itself has called for a renewed practice of baptism; and if we do not renew our practice of baptism, we will be unable to renew our understanding of baptism. How we celebrate even this "simple and insignificant" conclusion of the rite is important. There is more at stake here than meets the eye.

Notes

1. For a thorough analysis of this blessing, see Mark Searle's "Fons Vitae: A Case Study in the Use of Liturgy as a Theological Source," in *Fountain of Life*, ed. Gerard Austin (Washington DC: Pastoral Press, 1991), 217–42.

2. Annibale Bugnini, *The Reform of the Liturgy, 1948–1975*, trans. Matthew J. O'Connell (Collegeville: The Liturgical Press, 1990), 608.

3. Ibid., p. 608–609.

4. Ibid., p. 609.

Chapter 3

IN THE BEGINNING
WAS THE WORD

Baptism into Christ is anchored in our encounter with the living word. What St. Paul wrote a long time ago still holds true: "Faith comes from what is heard, and what is heard comes through the word of Christ." (Romans 10:17)

The *Rite of Christian Initiation of Adults* (RCIA) is explicit about this: The process of hearing and being formed by God's word is an absolute prerequisite for the sacramental rites. Those to be initiated must do what the entire church must do—be invited to faith by God's living word, by God who initiates this relationship called grace. They must listen and learn and be affected and wait. "The time spent in the catechumenate should be long enough for the conversion and faith of the catechumens to become strong." (RCIA, #76) "Among the rites belonging to the period of the catechumenate, celebrations of the word of God are foremost" (#79). There can be no sacrament, no life as sacrament, until and unless they and we "hear God's word and put it into action."

All the revised sacramental rites are clear and consistent about this: First comes the sharing of the word, and only then the sacramental action. No longer are the sacraments to be approached or celebrated as independent or autonomous or automatic events, but as responses to the word that invites us to faith.

What a change from the previous practice of infant baptism! The former rite, an abbreviated form of adult baptism, did not require or even provide for a sharing of the word. It was a disembodied rite, empowered to "cause what it signified," but in no sense a response to God's initiative and God's invitation. The sacramental action was the initiative of the church and of the family, sure to prevail upon God to do what was expected.

In contrast, the *Rite of Baptism for Children* (RBC), published in 1969, insists that the baptism is dependent upon the faith of the adult community, and that faith is to be centered in our encounter with God's word:

> The liturgy of the word is directed toward stirring up the faith of the parents, godparents and congregation, and praying in common for the fruits of baptism before the sacrament itself. (RBC, #17)

BAPTISM AT SUNDAY OR WEEKDAY MASS

When the baptism takes place at the Sunday liturgy, "the Mass for that Sunday is used, and . . . the readings are taken from the Mass of the Sunday, or, for special reasons, from those provided in the baptismal rite" (RBC, #29).

In practice, what might this mean? On Sundays, the readings prescribed for that day take precedence. This discipline helps the preacher and the assembly experience the cycle of the lectionary on a regular and persistent basis. "The choice and sequence of readings are aimed at giving the faithful an ever-deepening perception of the faith they profess and of the history of salvation." (*Lectionary for Mass: Introduction* [LMIn], #60)

Respecting the lectionary is one way for us to take the word on its own surprising terms instead of taking it on our terms. Following the Sunday lectionary teaches us to hear what God has to say or wishes to stir up for us, instead of deciding what we want God to say.

The Sunday liturgy, despite promotional materials indicating the contrary, is not a tool of Catholic Schools Week or National Migration Sunday. The Sunday liturgy of the word does not belong to the Campaign for Human Development or Respect Life Sunday or the Peter's Pence collection. "The decision was made [about the Sunday lectionary] . . . not to have an organic harmony of themes designed to aid homiletic instruction. . . . The liturgy is always a celebration of the mystery of Christ and makes use of the word of God on the basis of its own tradition." (LMIn, #68)

The readings assigned for the Sundays in Ordinary Time regularly lend themselves to the celebration of the rite of baptism. Typically, therefore, it is not necessary to ignore or change the lectionary texts to accommodate the rite of baptism to follow. This is the preference of the lectionary and of the rite of baptism as well.

But at other times, "for special reasons," it is helpful and fitting to substitute a reading from those suggested by the rite of baptism. For the sake of preaching about our baptismal life and celebration, for the edification of the assembly or for the benefit of a stronger link between the word proclaimed and the sacramental action to follow, it is sometimes helpful to use a reading or readings different from those that the lectionary provides.

When it is deemed necessary to substitute another reading, the simplest way is to replace the assigned epistle reading with another. This approach respects both the lectionary's progressive proclamation of the gospel and the connection of the gospel to the reading from the Hebrew scriptures ("The epistle and gospel readings are arranged in an order of semicontinuous reading, whereas the Old Testament reading is harmonized with the gospel." LMIn, #67). In addition, the epistles draw out the significance of baptism most explicitly. Various epistle excerpts provide the homilist and assembly ample foundation for the preaching and the ritual celebration to follow. Consider the epistles for the First Sunday of Lent in each of the three years of the lectionary cycle:

> **A)** Romans 5:12–19: "God's grace in Jesus Christ is far beyond the power of sin to which we are also born."

B) 1 Peter 3:18–22: an analogy between Noah and the ark and God's action now in baptism— "You are now saved by a baptismal bath which corresponds to this exactly."

C) Romans 10:8–13: "Confessing faith in Jesus Christ leads us to new life."

There are also some time-honored epistles, used at the Easter Vigil liturgies of the Eastern or the Western church to interpret the baptismal event:

- 1 Corinthians 15:1–11, already used by the year 440 at the Vigil in Jerusalem: "By the grace of God I am what I am, and God's grace toward me has not been in vain. . . . Whether then it was I or [the other apostles], so we proclaim and so you have come to believe."

- Colossians 3:1–4, used at the Easter Vigil in the Roman liturgy for more than 1400 years, from at least the sixth century until 1970: "Since you have been raised up in company with Christ, set your hearts on what pertains to higher realms. . . . After all, you have died!"

- Romans 6:3–11, used at the Great and Holy Saturday Vigil in the Orthodox liturgy; at the Royal Hours of Epiphany, the day when baptismal waters are blessed; and at all Orthodox celebrations of baptism throughout the year. The Roman Catholic liturgy of Easter Vigil has used this same epistle since 1970: "Are you not aware that we who were baptized into Christ Jesus were baptized into his death? Through baptism into his death we were buried with him, so that . . . we too might live a new life."

Generally, however, it is not necessary to substitute the lectionary's scheduled readings. For one thing, homilists need not preach as if the scripture texts were the only sources for explication. The homily "should develop some point of the readings or of another text from [the liturgy], and take into account the mystery being celebrated and the needs proper to the listeners" (*General Instruction of the Roman Missal*, #41). The celebration of baptism at the Sunday eucharist is a liturgical moment rich in homiletic possibilities. The liturgical event itself, the texts and the ritual elements of baptism all lend themselves appropriately and well to preaching. "The homily is based on the sacred texts, but should take account of the baptism which is to take place." (RBC, #29)

Second, there are few Sundays in the three-year cycle of readings when the celebration of baptism is completely incompatible or inappropriate to the scriptural texts. The perennial Sunday journey of encountering the word, responding with faith and moving to thanksgiving is the enduring story of baptismal faith.

The Sunday liturgy of the word is always intended to prompt faith. There need not be an explicit reference to baptism in any of the three readings for the Sunday lectionary and liturgy of the word to be quite suitable to the celebration of baptism. Nor should anyone insist that all three readings fit "a baptismal theme" to be suitable for celebrating baptism. That is a distortion of the Sunday lectionary and of the purpose of the liturgy of the word. Instead, baptismal faith and even the rite of baptism itself can spring from the typical Sunday liturgy of the word with little or no adjustment.

Third, the lectionary and liturgical calendar already provide some feasts and readings well suited to the celebration of baptism. Besides the Sundays in Ordinary Time, other Sundays and feasts almost suggest baptism. And the readings for these days help shape our church's baptismal life. For instance, consider some of these days and readings:

Epiphany: Isaiah 60:1–6; Ephesians 3:2–3, 5–6; Matthew 2:1–12. In the Orthodox liturgy, this feast remains the day for the blessing of the baptismal waters. The readings used at the Divine Liturgy are 1 Corinthians 9:19–27 and Luke 3:1–18; for the Blessing of the Water, Isaiah 35:1–10; Isaiah 12:3–6; Isaiah 55:1–13; 1 Corinthians 10:1–4; and Mark 1:9–11 are used.

Baptism of the Lord (Year A): Isaiah 42:1–4, 6–7; Acts 10:34–38; Matthew 3:13–17

Presentation of the Lord: Luke 2:22–40

Vigil of Easter

Easter Sunday: Acts 10:34, 37–43; Colossians 3:1–4 or 1 Corinthians 5:6–8; John 20:1–9 or the gospel from the Vigil

Other Sundays of Easter

Vigil of Pentecost: an ancient liturgy of baptism, whose readings used to be taken from those of the Easter Vigil. Now they include Romans 8:22–27 and John 7:37–39.

Pentecost: Acts 2:1–11; 1 Corinthians 12:3–7, 12–13; John 20:19–23

Birth of John the Baptist: Jeremiah 1:4–10; Isaiah 49:1–6; Luke 1:57–66, 80

Triumph of the Cross: Philippians 2:6–11; John 3:13–17

Feast of All Saints: 1 John 3:1–3; Matthew 5:1–12

Christ the King: Revelations 1:5–8 (Year B) and Colossians 1:12–20 (Year C)

This list could be expanded with little effort. The point is that the liturgical year and the lectionary already provide an ample framework for the public celebration of baptism. Rather than accommodating baptism on random Sundays, then shaping the lectionary to fit the schedule, parish communities would be better served by letting the lectionary and the calendar shape them and their rhythms of initiation. That in itself is a reminder of baptismal faith: learning to follow the Lord rather than trying to lead him.

Still another alternative presents itself. It may be deemed appropriate, when baptism will be a central element of both the preaching and the liturgy, to omit one of the readings (never the gospel). This may help both the preacher and the assembly to focus on the word more carefully and to give the baptism the time and attention it needs. More readings do not guarantee a better encounter with God's word, and the *Directory for Masses with Children* provides a rationale for this alternative: "In the choice of readings the criterion to be followed is the quality rather than the quantity of the texts from the scriptures." (#44)

For the typical parish community, the celebration of baptism at Mass on a weekday is a rare occurrence. When and if this occurs, the scripture readings may come either from the lectionary readings for the day, "or the readings may be taken from those that are provided in the rite of baptism" (RBC, #30). The preference, of course, is that baptism be celebrated on Sunday, "the original feast day, [when] the church celebrates the paschal mystery, the first day of the week."[1] The rite of baptism urges that baptism be associated with the Easter Vigil or with Sunday, the weekly celebration of Easter, "to bring out the paschal character of baptism" (RBC, #9).

When the rite of baptism is celebrated apart from Mass, the proclamation of the word remains a necessity. This liturgy of the word takes a simpler form than at the eucharistic liturgy; it is, however, no less significant. (Only in the most extreme cases is proclamation of the word ever omitted; see RBC, #21.)

> This part of the celebration [of the rite of baptism] consists of the reading of one or more passages from holy scripture; a homily, followed by a period of silence; the prayer of the faithful; and finally a prayer, drawn up in the style of an exorcism, to introduce either the anointing with the oil of catechumens or the laying on of hands. (RBC, #17)

The liturgy of the word begins with "the reading of one or more passages from holy scripture." Determining the number of readings is usually a pastoral judgment influenced by the noise level, the time of the liturgy, the disposition and size of the assembly and several other intangible factors. There may well be only one reading, with neither psalm nor gospel verse. But given the intended rhythm of the liturgy of the word—proclamation and response— and the role of music in liturgy ("The celebration of baptism is greatly enhanced by the use of song." RBC, #33), this is hardly the ideal.

A more appropriate minimal form would include an epistle reading; silent reflection; a psalm sung by cantor and assembly, or if there is no song leader, a familiar hymn based on a psalm; alleluia and gospel verse led by cantor, but omitted if there is no song leader; gospel passage.

The setting and context for this liturgy of the word are unusual and present special needs. Certainly, one would hope for the rapt attention of the adults. The rite, in its own clumsy way, makes this point:

When the liturgy of the word is being celebrated, it is desirable that the children should be taken to some other place. Provision should be made for the mothers or godmothers to attend the liturgy of the word; the children should therefore be entrusted to the care of other women. (RBC, #14)

The children to be baptized [then] may be carried to a separate place, where they remain until the end of the liturgy of the word. (RBC, #44)

But saying that the adults should not be distracted does not make it so. In the typical parish celebration of baptism with a small group, the parents and godparents are not single-mindedly focused on the word proclaimed and pondered. Sending the children off would be awkward, and is rarely done. The rite seems to acknowledge that this is not a typical liturgy of the word. For instance, "if circumstances permit" (#42), the word is to be proclaimed at the normal place. The word to be proclaimed may consist of "one or even two gospel passages," certainly an unusual arrangement. Even the characteristic posture for the proclamation of the gospel, standing, is negotiable: At this word service, "all may sit if convenient" (#44).

But the rite insists there must be a liturgy of the word, even if simpler and briefer than that of a Sunday or weekday eucharistic liturgy. Simple and brief it may be, but it is never intended to be perfunctory. At the least, there is to be "the reading of one or more passages from holy scripture and a homily, followed by a period of silence" (RBC, #17).[2]

CHOOSING READINGS There is great latitude in deciding on the reading(s) to be used at a baptism celebrated outside Mass. The rite explicitly presents three options in #44: one or two of the gospel texts printed in the body of the rite; passages from the lectionary for the baptism of children, which are reprinted at the end of the rite; "other passages which better meet the wishes or needs of parents." A fourth option, the readings of the Sunday, is also available.

1) *The gospels given in the text.* The rite first suggests four gospel pericopes—brief passages about the baptism of Jesus, the puzzlement of Nicodemus over a person being "born again," Jesus' insistence that the little children are models of faith, and his sending the disciples to preach and baptize.

2) *Passages from the lectionary for the baptism of children.* The rite provides a large selection of readings (#186–215) taken from the lectionary, any of which may be chosen. (This list is reprinted in the back of this book.) The list helps us recover and rediscover some far different approaches to baptism than we Western Christians are accustomed to. There are different theologies of baptism in the New Testament, some of which suit the baptism of children and infants better than others. These different theologies are not mutually exclusive, but rather are layers and developments. They represent a progression in under-standing as the early church's experience of baptism and initiation progressed.

Briefly, the early writings of St. Paul reflect what is called the "tomb theology" of baptism: Baptism means dying with Christ now so that we may share in the glory of Christ in the future. The death of Jesus was the turning point of salvation, which we identify with by "baptism into his death." Dying to the old is already underway, but rising to glory is not yet a reality:

> Do you not know that all of us who have been
> baptized into Christ Jesus were baptized into his
> death? Therefore we have been buried with him
> by baptism into death, so that, just as Christ was
> raised from the dead by the glory of the Father,
> so we too might walk in newness of life. For if we
> have been united with him in a death like his, we

77

will certainly be united with him in a resurrection like his. (Romans 6:3–5)

Later Pauline writings and deutero-Pauline writings (Colossians and Ephesians, for example) reflect a broader "dying and rising" theology of baptism. Those baptized already share in the resurrection life with Christ.

> When you were buried with him in baptism, you were also raised with him through faith in the power of God, who raised him from the dead. And when you were dead in trespasses and the uncircumcision of your flesh, God made you alive together with him, when he forgave us all our trespasses. (Colossians 2:12–13)

> You were dead. . . . But God, who is rich in mercy, out of the great love with which he loved us even when we were dead through our trespasses, made us alive together with Christ. . . . For by grace you have been saved through faith, and this is not your own doing; it is the gift of God, not the result of works, so that no one may boast. For we are what he has made us, created in Christ Jesus for good works, which God prepared beforehand to be our way of life. (Ephesians 2:1–10)

The later Acts of the Apostles, not represented in the rite's list of readings, reflects a rich "action of the Spirit" theology of baptism. Baptism manifests the action of the Spirit and means birth into *ekklesia,* into the Spirit-filled community. (This emphasis on the Spirit's presence and action permeates Acts, with nearly 60 references to the Spirit.)

> While Peter was still speaking [to Cornelius and his relatives and friends], the Holy Spirit fell upon all who heard the word. The circumcised believers who had come with Peter were astounded that the gift of the Holy Spirit had been poured out even on the Gentiles, for they heard them speaking in

tongues and extolling God. Then Peter said, "Can anyone withhold the water for baptizing these people who have received the Holy Spirit just as we have?" So he ordered them to be baptized in the name of Jesus Christ. Then they invited him to stay for several days. (Acts 10:44–48)

The Gospel of John represents another strain, a "womb" theology of baptism. It stresses "rebirth" and "adoption" dimensions of baptism and initiation, a perspective that is still somewhat foreign to us.

Now there was a Pharisee named Nicodemus, who came to Jesus by night and said to him, "Rabbi, we know that you are a teacher who has come from God. . . ." Jesus answered him, "Very truly, I tell you, no one can see the kingdom of God without being born from above." Nicodemus said, "How can anyone be born after having grown old? Can one enter a second time into the mother's womb and be born?" Jesus answered, "Very truly, I tell you, no one can enter the kingdom of God without being born of water and Spirit. . . . Do not be astonished that I said to you, You must be born from above. The wind blows where it chooses, and you hear the sound of it, but you do not know where it comes from or where it goes. So it is with everyone who is born of the Spirit." Nicodemus said, "How can these things be?" (John 3:1–10)

The subtleties of various baptismal theologies and images found in the New Testament may be lost on the average participant in a baptismal liturgy, but they should not be lost on the planners, presiders or homilists for baptism. The New Testament provides more theologies of baptism and far more images and models of baptism than we normally invoke. Utilizing a broader range of readings in the celebration of baptism can help develop a richer understanding of the sacrament.

For instance, a combination of the "tomb" theology of Pauline writings and the "dying and rising" theology of later epistles is a familiar and favored theology among Roman Catholics. It is especially fruitful as an explanation of the experience of adult initiation: leaving behind the old and taking up the new, identifying with the cross so as to share in the crown to come, choosing to turn toward Christ. (*The Rite of Christian Initiation of Adults* makes full use of this baptismal language and imagery.)

For nearly 1500 years, the rite for adult baptism, and the theology that suits that experience, was applied to infant baptism as well. But here, "dying to the old and rising to the new" does not fit so well. Infants and children do not have a lot of "dying to the old" to do, and the imagery limps. What filled the void was a theology and imagery of original sin, an "old life" even these youngsters can die to.

As of 1969, we have a rite for baptizing children and infants for the first time in the church's history. But we have not yet appropriated language and imagery suitable to this unique ritual experience. We still have a ritual experience that is wearing adult clothing in our minds. Worse, it is a ritual experience we approach after centuries of privatized and dismembered initiation. We are sorely in need of new perspectives to suit this new rite.

The challenge for planners, presiders and homilists is to make use of readings that cast this baptismal event in new light. New language and imagery will help us view the ritual experience in new ways, help us celebrate it in new ways, and so help us to understand it in new ways. The theology of dying and rising, the imagery of washing and the language of leaving original sin behind are not the mandatory or even the most traditional ways to frame this word service and ritual experience.

Surely the later theology of baptism as womb, the imagery of rebirth and adoption, and the understanding of baptism as the outpouring of the Holy Spirit more clearly align with the experience of baptizing infants and with the *Rite of Baptism for Children*.

For instance, highlighting baptism as "the great outpouring of the Holy Spirit" provides us with a different window on this ritual and with a new slant on the whole of initiation. Or viewing baptism primarily as "birth into the Spirit-filled community," a dominant image throughout Acts, offers a scriptural corrective to some of the impoverished language and images we still resort to, such as baptism as a "ritual cleansing," a "family celebration."

The great fourth-century preachers of initiation made full use of this theology and imagery. Ambrose, John Chrysostom, Cyril of Jerusalem and Theodore of Mopsuestia spoke at length about the font as womb, the baptism as birth, the baptism as the waters of creation stirred once again by God's spirit. As Jesus was generated in the womb of Mary by the Spirit, Ambrose preached, in the same way you are generated in the womb of the font by the action of the same Spirit.[3] John Chrysostom proclaimed that this baptism is spiritual child-bearing from the font, which is the womb of Mother Church.[4] By the Spirit, Theodore explains, the font becomes "a reverential womb for the second birth, so that those who descend . . . may be born again."[5] Such language and imagery, very traditional but less familiar to our Western ears, may be good lenses through which to choose and preach the scriptures for infant baptism.

Consider using the passage read every year on Pentecost, Acts 2:1–11. One can easily draw parallels between that story, the Spirit transforming the first disciples into the church, and the baptismal moment at hand, at which the newly baptized are born into the Spirit-filled community. Or use the reading the Orthodox church uses every year for its midnight Easter liturgy, Acts 1:1–8: "John baptized with water, but you will be baptized with the Holy Spirit." We have become church, it says, because Christ anoints us with his continuing presence. Or look closely at Mark 1:9–11, which recalls the wonders that sprang forth from Jesus' own baptism and anointing with the Spirit, and anticipate what will spring forth from the present baptism.

Or spend time with the seven passages from John's gospel that the rite suggests: Nicodemus wondering what rebirth is to mean; the Samaritan woman puzzling over the waters of life; Jesus declaring that all who believe will have new life; Jesus calling us to drink in the Spirit "which believers in him are to receive"; the blind man seeing and believing, and so God's saving action is revealed; Jesus proclaiming that God glories in the unity between himself and his disciples; the church being born from the side of the Crucified One, through the baptismal water and the eucharistic blood.

Even in planning for this word service, we face the very issues and changes in perspective this rite places before us. If the word service opens up some of this "new" language and imagery of womb and birth, then such robust elements as naked babies, the immersing of infants into the water, and the rich use of fragrant oil to anoint the royal heads begin to make sense.

3) *"Other passages which better meet the wishes or needs of the parents."* During baptismal preparation, parents and families can be provided with an expanded list of suggested readings and asked to help prepare for the word service. As is often done with engaged couples in preparation for wedding liturgy, so here the adults and children can be encouraged to spend time with the readings, write down their thoughts and reflections and provide these for the baptismal liturgy. Even if the presence of several families for the baptismal celebration precludes

each selecting the reading, their reflections on the deter-
mined reading or readings can benefit the homilist.

Or the parents and family can be invited to suggest other
scripture passages for the liturgy. This may require more
coordination and more preparation time than originally
planned. But it may enhance the word service for everyone involved. Other children in the household may already
have favorite Bible stories or figures to suggest and talk
about: the Spirit bringing forth life from the primordial
waters, the story of Noah, the passage of the Israelites
through the waters of the Red Sea, the baptism of Jesus.
Invitations to reflect on the scriptures or to suggest scripture passages also may provide a way for the parent or
family member who is not Catholic to help prepare for
the baptism.

The homilist is not the only person who benefits from
spending time with the scriptures; the word service is
enriched in direct proportion to the number of participants who have spent time reflecting on the scriptures in
light of the celebration to come.

4) *The readings from the Sunday liturgy.* If the baptism is celebrated shortly after the Sunday eucharist, the
epistle or gospel passage of that liturgy can be used for
the baptismal rite as well. This may help the presider and
homilist to link this baptismal celebration more directly
with the parish eucharist.

Notes

1. *General Norms for the Liturgical Year and the Calendar*, 4.

2. Annibale Bugnini, "Even after the rite had been published, there were calls for the elimination of the liturgy of the word," in *The Reform of the Liturgy, 1948–1975*, trans. Matthew J. O'Connell (Collegeville: The Liturgical Press, 1990), 606.

3. Ambrose, *De mysteriis*, 59.

4. John Chrysostom, *Baptismal Catechesis*, 4.1.

5. Theodore of Mopsuestia, *Mystagogical Writings*, Homily 3.10.

Chapter 4

THE CELEBRATION OF BAPTISM IS GREATLY ENHANCED BY SONG

The *Rite of Baptism for Children* spells out a dialogue, a "liturgical conversation" among those assembled. Very little of the rite is explicit prayer, language addressed to God. Rather, the majority of the rite consists of dialogue and shared actions by the presider, baptismal party and entire assembly. Notice how the rite engages all the participants (or intends to engage them), in dialogue fashion, in the words and actions of the rite.

Reception of the Children: The presider dialogues with the parents and godparents about intentions, expectations and intended meanings. After their give-and-take dialogue, they all join in the act of signing the child with the cross, an action easily extended to involve the entire baptismal party or small assembly.

Celebration of God's Word: The listening-responding pattern typical of the readings and psalm prevails. Everyone —assembly, family, presider—is engaged in this pattern, this dialogue with the word. Here there is equality as the entire body of people listens, reflects in silence, responds in psalmody or acclamation. Similarly, the litany of intercessions forms everyone into a single voice of rhythmic prayer, with its announcements of intentions to be prayed for and its response of prayer.

Celebration of the Sacrament: The blessing and invocation over the water is prayed by the presider in the name of all present ("We now ask God," "Let us ask God") and in the plural voice. In fact, forms B and C of the prayer are provided as litanies, with all joining in a repetitive response. The renunciation of sin and profession of faith are a dialogue between the baptismal party and presider, and might even involve the entire assembly. The actions of the baptismal bath and anointing with chrism are done by the presider; the lesser actions of clothing with the garment and lighting the baptismal candle are done by members of the baptismal party.

Conclusion of the Rite: The baptismal party and presider, at least, gather by the altar, and the entire assembly prays the Lord's Prayer together. The blessings are presented as dialogues with responses by all; the accompanying action may involve all present, who may extend hands over the baptismal party.

This is a different perspective on the rite than is normally encountered, and it is a different perspective than what one often sees in practice. But it is not stretching things to say that the rite is intended to be an engaging, inclusive dialogue. The bulk of the rite consists of dialogues between the presider and the baptismal party (and to a lesser extent the entire assembly) and of actions involving the presider (and to a lesser extent the baptismal party, and to an even lesser extent the assembly).

The rite encourages us to approach it as a living dialogue by encouraging the presider to use the rite as a model rather than as a script: "The celebrant may choose other words for [the opening] dialogue." "The parents may use other words." "The celebrant speaks to the parents in these or similar words." "The celebrant addresses [the godparents] in these or similar words." Such suggestions are given throughout the rite; even the General Introduction urges the presiders and planners to use their good judgment in shaping this dialogue of words and actions: "The ministers, taking into account circumstances and needs, as well as the wishes of the faithful, should use the various choices allowed in the rite." (# 34)

THE VOICE OF THE ASSEMBLY

Even though the majority of the dialogue and the majority of the actions involve primarily the presider and the baptismal party, the rite insists that the entire assembly be engaged. There are ways the assembly can be drawn more fully into some of the actions of the rite, such as the signing of the children with the cross, and the final blessing. Similarly, the entire assembly can be drawn more fully into some of the words of the rite, such as the renunciation of sin and the profession of faith.

But the "active participation" expected of the assembly does not mean that everyone must do everything. A thousand people cannot help dress the child, nor can a congregation of even 450 process to the altar for the conclusion. "Active participation" means *attentive* participation: attentive *listening*, attentive *viewing*, attentive *standing*, attentive *recitation*, even attentive *silence* and *reflection*. It means participating as a collective body, participating with our attention focused. Attentive participation means that the role of the assembly in the dialogue of the rite is central to the worship, that the baptism is celebrated by and with and for the assembly.

To draw the assembly into this ritual dialogue as a full, conscious and active celebrant, the rite says that singing is the surest way.

> The celebration of baptism is greatly enhanced by the use of song. It stimulates a sense of unity among those present, it gives warmth to their common prayer, and it expresses the joy of Easter. [Especially needed are] settings for texts suitable for congregational singing at baptism. (GI, #33)

The *Rite of Baptism for Children* calls for song throughout the celebration. Congregational singing is the assembly's voice, the way the assembly converses with the words and actions of the rite. Singing is the fullest way the assembly joins the presider and baptismal party as an equal partner in the dialogue the rite envisions. Notice all the points at which the rite suggests music be employed:

RECEPTION OF THE CHILD
Gathering Music: As the ministers process to the doors to greet the baptismal party, "the people may sing a psalm or hymn suitable for the occasion" (#35).

Music with the Procession: As ministers and baptismal party move for the liturgy of the word, "there is a procession . . . during which a song is sung, e.g., Psalm 84:7– 9ab" (#42).

CELEBRATION OF GOD'S WORD
Psalmody: "Between the readings, responsorial psalms or verses may be sung as given in numbers 195–197 [Psalm 23, Psalm 27, Psalm 34]." (#44)

Hymn: "After the homily . . . or after the litany, a period of silence while all pray. . . . If convenient, a suitable song follows, e.g., from numbers 225–245" (#46).

Music with the Procession: As all or some process to the baptistry or place for baptism, "if it can be done suitably, an appropriate song is sung, e.g., Psalm 23" (# 52).

CELEBRATION OF THE SACRAMENT
Blessing of God over Baptismal Water: In form B or C of the prayer, various acclamations may be sung by all (#54).

Profession of Faith: The assembly affirms the profession of faith in dialogue with the presider, or by means of "a suitable song by which the community expresses its faith with a single voice" (#59).

Baptism: The assembly responds to the baptismal action by song: "After each baptism it is appropriate for the people to sing a short acclamation." (#60)

MUSIC WITH THE CONCLUSION OF THE RITE
Procession: As all or some process toward the altar, "a baptismal song is appropriate" (#67).

Lord's Prayer: "All join the celebrant in singing or saying. . . . "(#68)

Conclusion: "All may sing a hymn which suitably expresses thanksgiving and Easter joy, or they may sing . . . the Magnificat." (#71)

SOME PRACTICAL SUGGESTIONS Music serves a pragmatic purpose in the rite, filling in the time needed to move people from one point to another (the processions). But more significantly, music enhances certain words and actions (the profession of faith, the baptism) for the assembly. Music also enables the entire assembly to participate vicariously (or attentively) in parts of the rite (the processions, standing at the altar). As always in our liturgy, music forms everyone present into one voice, one body ("stimulates a sense of unity among those present"), thus helping everyone to say and to do what only a few are actually saying and doing. Music helps everyone process (as only a few actually do so), helps everyone pray over the waters (as only one actually does so), helps everyone lift the child out of the waters (as only a few hands actually do so). Music is the robust voice of the assembly in the dialogue of the rite.

In practice, this "voice of the assembly" is not utilized well. In the smaller parish celebration of infant baptism, with only one or a few family groups present, music is almost never used. The rite remains a series of actions done primarily by the presider—more a monologue than dialogue. When baptism is celebrated at Sunday Mass, it seldom receives special musical attention at all. The music already in place for the Sunday eucharist suffices. So the congregation, not given its voice and part in the rite, rightly complains that the baptism is both verbose and an intrusion—"it doesn't involve us." In either setting, without this voice of the assembly, the ritual is weakened and the baptism remains more something we watch than something we do.

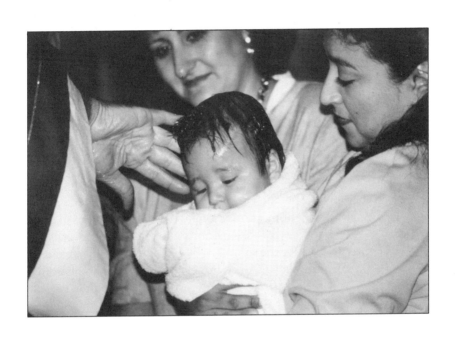

There are simple ways to use music in celebrating baptism with both large and small groups. For instance, consider how to incorporate the baptism and its music more closely into Sunday Mass:

- The congregation sings one or two verses of the first hymn as ministers process to the doors. Once the greeting and signing with the cross are finished, all sing the rest of the same hymn as the baptismal party moves to their places in the assembly.

- The psalm and gospel acclamation are sung as usual. A brief litany of the saints is sung by all after the prayers of the faithful as the procession moves toward the font or place of baptism.

- The "Celebration of the Sacrament" stands to benefit most from simple music. Look at obvious sources for acclamations: the music the parish uses for the sprinkling rite; the sung prayers, psalms and acclamations from the Easter Vigil and Easter Sunday liturgies; a response the parish already sings with Psalms 23, 34, 42, 63, 84. The sprinkling rite, the Easter Vigil and baptisms are regular features of parish liturgy, and all of them require similar music. Utilizing the same pieces with all these will simplify things for everyone, and utilizing short acclamations will work better than hymns. A sung acclamation with the blessing over the water, with the profession of faith, and with each baptism can intensify each element and draw the assembly into it.

- The Lord's Prayer might be sung at this Sunday Mass, perhaps as a consistent feature with all parish baptisms. A final hymn expressing our baptismal life and discipleship is sung by all.

Even a smaller gathering can greatly benefit from the use of music for this liturgy. The Rite of Baptism for Children reminds us that the real model for the baptismal liturgy is not the single-family baptism, nor is this practice to be encouraged anymore. It should be a "communal celebration for all recently born children and in the presence of the faithful" (RBC, #32). Why this call for a change in our pastoral practice? Precisely because the liturgical experience needs to be more communal, richer, fuller than when baptism is meted out one infant at a time. The church gathered needs a better liturgy than that! "The church has a right to the full celebration of its own rites."

Even when a small group gathers for baptism (a family group of seven people, for instance), singing can greatly enrich the experience and can be provided for quite easily.

> ■ Begin with one or two verses of a hymn everyone will know by heart: a seasonal hymn, an Easter hymn, a hymn of praise. Use one that grandparents or friends who are Protestants can easily join in singing. It's a delight if the baptism is celebrated in the Christmas Season, when people know many seasonal hymns.

> ■ Depending on the simplicity of the liturgy of the word and on the number of readings to be used, the cantor can lead everyone in a responsorial psalm. At the least, even with a group of seven people, sing a gospel acclamation. A simple "Alleluia" helps the group focus on the reading instead of the crying infant.

> ■ Use an acclamation with the blessing and with the baptism; the same one may even be used for both. Borrow one from the parish Easter Vigil or use the one the parish uses with the sprinkling rite. Remember that the Easter Vigil, the sprinkling rite and rite of baptism all use the same blessing prayer. All these occasions can benefit from the use of the same sung acclamations.

■ With everyone gathered around the altar for the conclusion, finish with a hymn everyone knows. Again, use one everybody can sing by heart, perhaps even a verse of the same hymn used earlier.

YES, IT CAN BE DONE

Do you still think that singing will never work at your parish's baptisms? Don't be so sure. More than likely, the real problem is not the rite's call for music but the parish's approach to its baptisms. Does the parish still celebrate only one baptism at a time? It's hard for a group of seven people, for instance, to sing well in a large church building; if 40 people are gathered, then singing is easier and more necessary. More and more parishes celebrate baptism on a less frequent basis to ensure a significant number present for this parish liturgy, as the rite insists. Does the parish involve a musician, cantor and other ministers in baptisms outside Mass? Or does the priest or deacon still function as the only true minister for this parish liturgy? In far too many parishes, baptism is still something the priest or deacon does, serving as greeter, lector, song leader and presider. This guarantees that "singing will never work," but is hardly the picture of a renewed and restored initiation liturgy.

Too often the problem is not that "music will never work," but that the parish practice of infant baptism has not changed. The *Rite of Baptism for Children* calls for a reform of our baptismal practices. It intends this to be a true liturgy of the parish, with the same standards of celebration and participation as other liturgies of the parish. It intends singing to be one means to a more balanced and appropriate celebration, in which the assembly, large or small, finds its full and equal part in this celebration of its faith.

Appendix 1

SCRIPTURAL TEXTS FOR USE IN THE CELEBRATION OF BAPTISM FOR CHILDREN

I n preparation for baptism, the family may be invited to read the following scripture passages and select some for the baptismal liturgy, "or other passages which better meet the wishes or needs of the parents may be chosen" (RBC, #44).

FROM THE *RITE OF BAPTISM FOR CHILDREN*:

Exodus 17:3–7: Water from the rock

Ezekiel 36:24–28: Clean water, a new heart, a renewed spirit

Ezekiel 47:1–9, 12: The water of salvation

Romans 6:3–5: Baptism: a sharing in Christ's death and resurrection

Romans 8:28–32: We have become more perfectly like God's own Son.

1 Corinthians 12:12–13: Baptized in one Spirit to form one body

Galatians 3:26–28: Now that you have been baptized you have put on Christ.

Ephesians 4:1–6: One lord, one faith, one baptism

1 Peter 2:4–5, 9–10: A chosen race, a royal priesthood

Psalm 23: The Lord is my shepherd, there is nothing I shall want.

Psalm 27: The Lord is my light and my salvation.

Psalm 34: Come to him and receive his light.

Matthew 22:35–40: The first and most important commandment

Matthew 28:18–20: Christ sends his apostles to teach and baptize.

Mark 1:9–11: The baptism of Jesus

Mark 10:13–16: Jesus loves children

Mark 12:28–34: Love God with all your heart.

John 3:1–6: The meeting with Nicodemus

John 4:5–14: Jesus speaks with the Samaritan woman.

John 6:44–47: Eternal life through belief in Jesus

John 7:37–39: Streams of living water

John 9:1–7: Jesus heals a blind man who believes in him.

John 15:1–11: Union with Christ, the true vine

John 19:31–35: The death of Christ, the witness of John
the apostle

ADDITIONAL READINGS

The list of readings in the rite can be supplemented by
other readings from the lectionary.

EPIPHANY
Roman Catholic lectionary: Isaiah 60:1–6;
Ephesians 3:2–3, 5–6; Matthew 2:1–12

Orthodox Divine Liturgy: 1 Corinthians 9:19–27;
Luke 3:1–18

Orthodox Blessing of the Water: Isaiah 35:1–10;
Isaiah 12:3–6; Isaiah 55:1–13; 1 Corinthians 10:1–4;
Mark 1:9–11

BAPTISM OF THE LORD
Matthew 3:13–17 (Year A); Luke 3:15–22 (Year C)

PRESENTATION OF THE LORD
Luke 2:22–40

VIGIL OF EASTER
Roman Catholic lectionary: Genesis 1:1—2:2;
Exodus 14:15—15:1; Isaiah 55:1–11; Ezekiel 36:16–28

Orthodox midnight Easter Vigil liturgy: Acts 1:1–8

EASTER SUNDAY
Acts 10:34, 37–43; Colossians 3:1—4;
1 Corinthians 5:6–8; John 20:1–9 or the gospel from
the Vigil

VIGIL OF PENTECOST
Romans 8:22–27 and John 7:37–39

PENTECOST
Acts 2:1–11; 1 Corinthians 12:3–7, 12–13;
John 20:19–23

BIRTH OF JOHN THE BAPTIST
Jeremiah 1:4–10; Isaiah 49:1–6; Luke 1:57–66, 80

TRIUMPH OF THE CROSS
Philippians 2:6–11; John 3:13–17

FEAST OF ALL SAINTS
1 John 3:1–3 and Matthew 5:1–12

CHRIST THE KING
Revelation 1:5–8 (Year B); Colossians 1:12–20 (Year C)

Appendix 2

PRAYERS AND BLESSINGS

Two sources for prayer, blessings and help with pastoral visits, the *Book of Blessings* and *Catholic Household Blessings and Prayers*, are helpful for both parish personnel and individual households. These books can be drawn upon to assist in the pastoral care, family prayer and general parish hospitality surrounding the childbirth, the family's preparation for baptism and the celebration of the baptism.

Both the *Book of Blessings*, designed for more formal use on the parish level, and *Catholic Household Blessings and Prayers*, designed for use by individual families and households, provide resources that are flexible and timely.

CATHOLIC HOUSEHOLD BLESSINGS AND PRAYERS

Published by the National Conference of Catholic Bishops, Bishops' Committee on the Liturgy (BCL), Washington, DC, 1988.

The hardbound edition costs approximately $20; a paperback edition is available for less. A copy of this book might be presented to the family by the parish during a visit prior to baptism for a newborn child, or at the time of the baptism. The book includes many resources for prayer that parents, godparents and parishioners involved in baptismal preparation or in a visit to the new parents can use. These include:

> Blessing for the conception or adoption of a child, page 215

> Blessing during pregnancy:
> for both parents, page 217
> for the mother, page 220

> Blessing near the time of birth, page 223

> Thanks for a newborn or newly adopted child, page 224

Parents' thanksgiving, page 225

Blessing on bringing a child into a home, page 226

Mother's blessing of a child when nursing or feeding, page 226

Blessing of parents after a miscarriage, page 277

BOOK OF BLESSINGS   Prepared by the International Commission on English in the Liturgy (ICEL) and published by Catholic Book Publishing Company (New York) and The Liturgical Press (Collegeville MN), 1989.

This is the ritual for the formal blessings by the church. It contains many resources for use around pregnancy, childbirth, baptism of children, sudden death of a child, or adoption of a child. Its suggestions can help parish personnel prepare blessings and public prayer that seek God's care for parents, infants and households. The suggestions include:

Order for the blessing of baptized children, page 73

Order for the blessing of a child not yet baptized, page 80

Order for the blessing of parents before childbirth, page 102

Orders for the blessing of a mother before childbirth and after childbirth, page 110

Order for the blessing of parents after a miscarriage, page 125

Order for the blessing of parents and an adopted child, page 133

Other Related Materials from
Liturgy Training Publications:

In English:

A Baptism Sourcebook
edited by J. Robert Baker, Larry Nyberg and Victoria
M. Tufano
> An anthology of fiction, poetry, theological
> texts, hymn texts related to baptism.
> *Order code:* BAPTSB

The Godparent Book
by Elaine Ramshaw
> Suggestions for building the bond between
> godparent and godchild.
> *Hardcover order code:* H/GPBK
> *Paperback order code:* GPBOOK

A Place for Baptism
by Regina Kuehn
> An illustrated exploration of the meaning
> of baptism through the design of baptistries.
> *Order code:* BPLACE

Baptism Is a Beginning edited by Rebekah Rojcewicz
A Four-year Series for Parish and Parents
> Fourteen handouts designed to support the
> parish's baptism-preparation program.
> *Sample packet order code:* BBNEW

New Life: A Parish Celebrates Infant Baptism
> A video of a parish's celebration of the Rite of
> Baptism for Children during Sunday liturgy.
> *VHS order code:* LIFE

Catechesis and Mystagogy: Infant Baptism

A discussion of the pastoral care of families before and after the baptism of their infants.
Order code: CATMYS

The Religious Potential of the Child
by Sofia Cavalletti

Discusses the spiritual growth of the young children.
Order code: CHILD

The Good Shepherd and the Child
by Sofia Cavalletti, Particia Coulter, Gianna Gobbi and Silvana Q. Montanaro

Instruction for implementing the Catechesis of the Good Shepherd.
Order code: GSHEP

Baptismal Certificates
Call for descriptions.

In Spanish:

El Bautismo de los Niños

Spanish edition of *Baptism Is a Beginning.*
Order code: ELBAU

Preparación para el Bautismo

A guide for those who prepare parents for their child's baptism.
Order code: PBAU

Baptismal Certificates
Call for descriptions.

The act of baptizing is essential to the church's life. Yet all too often the baptism of infants is a private, hurried ritual. This book challenges everyone who prepares the liturgy of infant baptism to understand it as the action of the community that begets new believers and nurtures the faith of those it begets. Timothy Fitzgerald applies the standards of the liturgical reform—the full, conscious and active participation of the assembly; the word proclaimed and preached; the integration of music and ritual; the abundant use of symbols, gestures and movements—to the *Rite of Baptism for Children*. Whether it is celebrated at the Sunday eucharist or at a separate assembly, infant baptism is a parish celebration.

Timothy Fitzgerald is a priest of the diocese of Des Moines, Iowa. He has served in parish ministry and adult education and writes regularly on issues of pastoral liturgy. He has earned a master of arts in theology at the University of Louvain, Belgium, and a master of arts in liturgical studies at the University of Notre Dame. He is associate director of the Notre Dame Center for Pastoral Liturgy.

LTP

INBAPR

$8.95

Font and Table Series

WACKY WEDNESDAY

By Theo. LeSieg

Illustrated by
George Booth

_____

(YOUR NAME HERE)

Kellogg's®

LOOK INTO BOOKS!
With Dr. Seuss And Friends!

reading program

® Kellogg Company